Unmarried Parents' Rights

2nd Edition

Jacqueline D. Stanley
Attorney at Law

SPHINX® PUBLISHING
AN IMPRINT OF SOURCEBOOKS, INC.®
NAPERVILLE, ILLINOIS
www.SphinxLegal.com

Copyright © 1999, 2003 by Jacqueline D. Stanley
Cover and internal design © 2003 by Sourcebooks, Inc.®

Second Edition, 2003
Published by: **Sphinx® Publishing, An Imprint of Sourcebooks, Inc.®**

<u>Naperville Office</u>
P.O. Box 4410
Naperville, Illinois 60567-4410
630-961-3900
Fax: 630-961-2168
www.sourcebooks.com
www.SphinxLegal.com

This publication is designed to provide accurate and authoritative information in
regard to the subject matter covered. It is sold with the understanding that the publisher is not engaged in rendering legal, accounting, or other professional service. If
legal advice or other expert assistance is required, the services of a competent professional person should be sought.
From a Declaration of Principles Jointly Adopted by a Committee of the
American Bar Association and a Committee of Publishers and Associations

This product is not a substitute for legal advice.
Disclaimer required by Texas statutes.

Library of Congress Cataloging-in-Publication Data
Stanley, Jacqueline D.
   Unmarried parents' rights / by Jacqueline D. Stanley. - - 2nd ed.
      p. cm.
   Includes index.
   ISBN 1-57248-236-2 (pbk.)
   1. Single parents - -Legal status, laws, etc. - -United States - -Popular works.
I. Title.
KF547.z9 s73 2002
346.7301'7 - -dc21

                                                                    2002012178

Printed and bound in the United States of America.

VHG Paperback — 10 9 8 7 6 5 4 3 2 1

CONTENTS

INTRODUCTION

This book is *designed* to be a practical, "how-to" guide for people who have children born out-of-wedlock. It will help you to understand and protect your legal rights, whether you decide to act on your own or through a lawyer.

Although this book is not designed for divorced parents, most of the legal concepts relating to child custody, visitation, and support will also apply to divorced parents. Step-parents are a unique class and their much more limited rights are beyond the scope of this book.

I have dispensed with as much legal jargon and legal theory as possible. There will be no discussion of what the law *should* be. This book is a practical guide to what the law is, and how the system works.

PARENTAL RIGHTS

There are two basic sources of parental rights:

1. the United States Constitution, and
2. the laws of the various states.

Each of these sources are supplemented by decisions of federal and state courts.

When the founding fathers outlined the rules that would govern this country, they wanted to be sure to limit the authority given to the federal government. If you think about the reason this country was formed, that makes sense. The people who formed this country wanted to create a government that would not unduly intrude into the private lives and homes of its citizens. That is why the

Constitution has provisions which protect an individual's privacy and freedom to associate with whomever they choose. This means the government cannot dictate who we should marry. And, as long as there is no abuse or neglect, the government cannot interfere with how we raise our children.

The second source of parental rights is the statutes, or laws, enacted by state legislatures. The U.S. Constitution only sets forth general principles of individual freedom, which have been interpreted to give parents a right to a certain degree of privacy with their children. Within these Constitutional limits, each state has the authority to develop laws and procedures that pertain to the relationship between a parent and child. For example, each state may determine how paternity can be established; how a judge must go about determining custody; and, under what circumstances parental rights can be limited or terminated.

This means that a parent in one state might enjoy more, or different, rights than a parent in another state. However, the statutes enacted by a state cannot infringe on a parent's rights under the U.S. Constitution. Although the rights under the Constitution are not specifically stated, parental rights are derived from the Fourth Amendment, which protects an individual's right to privacy.

While it is true that rights vary from state to state, there are three things that are fairly consistent throughout this country:

(1) parents have a right to a relationship with their children, either in the form of custody or visitation,

(2) parents have a duty to financially support their children to the extent they are able to do so, and

(3) a parent cannot abuse or neglect his or her child. This book is designed to guide you through the process of finding out what your rights are, and then enforcing them if necessary.

Parental rights generally encompass one, or a combination of the following:

- the right to care for your child;
- the right to have physical possession or custody of your child;
- the right to control or determine what is best for your child;

- the right to control with whom your child will associate and where your child will live;
- the right to decide where and how your children will be educated;
- the right to make health and medical decisions on behalf of your child;
- the right to determine your child's religious faith and practices; and,
- the right to provide guidance and discipline.

This does not mean that you have the right to do whatever you want with your children. Up to a point, parents have the right to exercise care, custody, and control over their children. Their rights can be restricted by state laws designed to protect children from abuse or neglect. One parent's rights might also be encumbered by the other parent's rights. For example, one parent's right to physical possession of his or her child can be encumbered by the other parent's right to weekend or summer visitation. However, under normal circumstances, parents who act reasonably will be free from government interference.

Legally, parental rights for mothers begin at the moment of conception. An unmarried father's rights begin at the moment paternity is established, and in some instances at the moment the father has reason to believe he is the parent and begins taking action to enforce his rights (which can also be immediately after conception).

Parents do not have to go to court to *obtain* their rights. They have rights merely by their status as parents. However, they might have to go to court to *enforce* those rights, and this can be a long, uphill battle.

HOW TO USE THIS BOOK

Begin by reading the book from cover-to-cover. This will help you determine what is relevant to your situation and what is not relevant. A cover-to-cover reading will also help you distinguish what you think you already know, from what the law really is. It will also make clear what you don't know and help you determine when you may need to go to a lawyer, the office of the clerk of court, or the law library.

Remember, the greatest threat to your rights as a parent is not knowing your rights. The second greatest threat is your failure to take action to enforce your rights. Keep reading and I can begin to help you overcome the first threat. Overcoming the second threat is up to you.

Chapter 1 discusses your general responsibilities as a parent, either married or unmarried. Chapter 2 explains the basics of the legal system as it relates to unmarried parents. It can help you obtain further information about the laws and procedures that are unique to your state. Chapter 3 will help you decide if you want to hire a lawyer. If so, the information witll help you work with your lawyer more effectively. Chapters 4 and 5 discuss legal forms and court procedures that are common to all types of legal matters relating to unmarried parents. Chapters 6 through 10 explains in greater detail the various types of legal proceedings relating to unmarried parents.

An extensive Glossary helps you understand the meanings of legal terms that may be unfamiliar. Appendix A contains a state-by-state summary of the relevant laws. Appendix B contains sample filled-in forms. Appendix C is a list of valuable extensive resources.

–1–
PARENTAL RESPONSIBILITIES

The legal responsibilities placed on parents for their children are enormous. These obligations are basically the same for married parents, divorced parents, and parents who have never been married. Parental duties are among the many factors you should consider before taking any action to establish paternity or file for custody or visitation.

The most obvious of legal parental responsibilities are providing children with adequate food, clothing, and shelter; as well as appropriate medical treatment and access to public, private, or home school instruction. However, other responsibilities may not be as obvious.

YOUR CHILD'S MISCONDUCT

Many states have enacted laws that hold parents directly responsible for the conduct or misconduct of their children. The following are examples of children's conduct for which parents are held responsible:

- curfew violations;
- school truancy (failing to attend school on a regular basis);
- weapon and firearm violations;
- vandalism;
- gang-related activity; and,
- drug and alcohol-related activity.

The punishments imposed on parents can include jail sentences; fines of $100 to $25,000 (depending on the state and the violation); and being ordered to attend family counseling and classes on parenting.

States have taken action to hold parents responsible for the misconduct of their children in reaction to the drastic increase in the rate of criminal activity by juveniles. Many believe the increase is due, in part, to parents' failure to control and discipline their children. Therefore, it is believed that holding parents responsible is a way to encourage them to take responsibility for their children's conduct.

There may be nothing that a parent can do to avoid being held responsible for their child's conduct. However, since a parent's liability is based on their failure to control and discipline their children, following these steps might minimize your liability.

- Do not ignore early warning signs that your child might be headed for trouble. According to researchers, these signs include a child whose grades suddenly drop, or who loses interest in activities they once enjoyed and friends with whom they once associated.

   For example, if your child comes home with expensive shoes, clothes, stereo equipment, etc., yet has no reasonable explanation of where the items came from or how the child can afford them, this could indicate that your child is engaged in illegal activity.

- Intervene at the first hint of trouble or inappropriate conduct. Contact your child's school counselor about guidance on where you should turn for help.
- Keep written records of whatever steps you take to assist your child. This information might be useful to you if you are ever charged with failing to prevent or intervene on behalf of your troubled child.

   For example, write down every time you contact social services about parenting classes or consult with the police about the warning signs of drug abuse.

- Do what you can to prevent trouble. Spend time with your children. Get them involved in organized sports or whatever other activities they enjoy. Stay involved in your children's lives and make sure you know who their friends are and what they are doing when they are not around you.

◆ Learn as much as you can about being an effective parent. Take classes, attend seminars, and join support groups that can assist you in raising your children.

PHYSICAL DISCIPLINE

You can use physical force to discipline and control your children, as long as it is appropriate, reasonable, and does not cross over into abuse. The following may be identified as signs that your method of physical discipline is not reasonable.

◆ You use something other than your open hand.

◆ You hit the child anywhere other than on their rear end.

◆ You leave marks or bruises on the child.

◆ You hit the child out of anger.

◆ You hit the child while you are under the influence of drugs or alcohol.

YOUR CHILD'S DEBTS

You are not responsible for the debts your children incur. For example, if your minor child goes out and orders $1,000 worth of baseball cards from a mail order catalog, you will not be responsible for paying the bill when it arrives. Ordinarily, contracts entered into by children are not legally binding. This means children cannot be forced to pay for items they have agreed to buy. If they cannot be forced to pay, neither can you. They can be forced to return the items they order. The only exception concerns items necessary for children's health and welfare. Parents can be held responsible for paying for these items.

CUSTODIAL VS. NON-CUSTODIAL PARENT LIABILITY

Generally, whichever parent has control of the children will be held responsible for their conduct.

Consider this example: William and Whitney had two children. They were never married but shared the responsibility for caring for the children. The children live the majority of the time with their mother. During a weekend visitation with William, one of the older children took one of his guns and shot a neighbor, paralyzing him.

Parents are not automatically held responsible in these situations. Whether William is held responsible in this case depends on the following three questions:

1. Did William follow state law in maintaining the weapon? Some states require guns to be locked up in households where there are likely to be children around.

2. Was the child being properly supervised at the time he gained access to the gun?

3. Did William have reason to know that the child might use the weapon and fail to do anything to prevent the problem?

Whitney's responsibility may turn on whether she knew there might be a problem with the child using the weapon while in William's care and whether she could have done anything to prevent it.

The bottom line is that the facts of each case will dictate the level of a parent's liability. That is why it is difficult to make predictions. You should know that both the custodial and non-custodial parent could be responsible for their child's conduct.

DURATION OF RESPONSIBILITY

A parent will be responsible for the conduct of their children until the first occurrence of one of the following events.

◆ The child reaches the age of majority, which typically ranges from sixteen to twenty depending upon the state.

◆ The parents' rights are terminated by a court.

◆ The child is no longer in the parents' custody. (If the child is not in your legal custody, it is assumed you have no control over the child's conduct. Remember, holding parents responsible for their children's behavior is based on a parent's inability or refusal to take control.)

◆ The child is taken into custody by a child protective agency.

◆ The child becomes emancipated, which means the child is legally recognized as an adult. This can happen if:

- The child marries. (If a child enters into a valid marriage, most states will recognize that as the child's emancipation.)

- The child joins the military.

- The child is emancipated through court action. (In some states, a child can file a court proceeding asking to be emancipated. Most states have a minimum age at which a child can file. The child must be mature enough to be financially self-sufficient. You cannot emancipate a child simply by putting him or her out of your home, even if they are self-supporting. You might still be responsible for his or her conduct, despite removing the child from your home. You may run the risk of being charged with neglect or abuse by the state child welfare agency.)

–2–
THE LEGAL SYSTEM AND UNMARRIED PARENTS

There are things you need to know about the legal system in order to enforce your rights and get through any encounter with the system with a minimum of stress. This chapter will give you a general introduction to the legal system. It will also discuss how the system is supposed to work, and some of the realities of our system. If you do not learn to accept these realities, you will have to accept the fact that you are setting yourself up for a great deal of frustration.

THEORY VS. REALITY
Our legal system is a system of three types of rules:

1. *Rules of Law*—These provide the basic substance of the law, such as a law stating how a judge must go about deciding which parent should be awarded custody.

2. *Rules of Procedure*—These outline how matters are to be handled in the courts, such as requiring court papers to be in a certain form, or filed within a specific time.

3. *Rules of Evidence*—These require facts to be proven in a certain way.

The theory is that these rules allow each side to present evidence most favorable to their side, and an independent person or persons (the judge, or jury in cases which permit a jury) will be able to figure out the "truth." Then, certain legal principles will be applied to that truth which will result in a fair resolution of the dispute between the parties.

These legal principles are supposed to be relatively unchanging so that we can all know what will happen in any given situation and can plan our lives accordingly. These guidelines will provide order and predictability to our society. Any change in the legal principles is supposed to occur slowly, so that the expected behavior in our society is not confused from day to day.

Unfortunately, the system doesn't really work this way. What follows are only some of the problems in the legal system.

The System is Not Perfect

Contrary to how it may seem, legal rules are not made just to complicate the system and confuse everyone. They are attempts to make the system as fair and just as possible. These rules have been developed over several hundred years, and in most cases they make sense. Unfortunately, our efforts to find fairness and justice have resulted in a complex set of rules. The legal system affects our lives in important ways; it is not a game. However, it can be compared to a game in some ways. The rules are designed to apply to all people, in all situations. The rules don't always give a fair result; however, they are still followed. Just as a referee can make a bad call, so can a judge. There are also cases where one side wins by cheating.

Judges Do Not Always Follow the Rules

This is a shocking discovery for many young lawyers. After spending three years in law school learning legal theory, countless hours preparing for a hearing, and having all of the law on your side, you find that the judge is not going to pay any attention to legal theories and the law. Many judges are going to make a decision simply on what they think "seems fair" under the circumstances. This concept is actually being taught in some law schools.

Unfortunately, what seems fair to a particular judge may depend upon her personal ideas and philosophy. For example, there is nothing in many states' custody laws that gives one parent priority in child custody cases; however, a majority of judges believe that a young child is generally better off with its mother. All other things being equal, these particular judges will find a way to justify awarding custody to the mother, even if it means twisting the law or the facts.

The System is Often Slow

Even lawyers get frustrated at how long it can take to get a case completed (especially if they do not get paid until it is done). Whatever your situation, things will take longer than you expect. Patience is required to get through the system with a minimum of stress. Do not let your impatience or frustration show. No matter what happens, keep calm, and be courteous and polite to the judge, to the court clerks, to any lawyers involved, and even to the opposing party (at least while you are in court).

No Two Cases are Alike

Just because your friend's case went a certain way does not mean yours will have the same result. The judge can make a difference, and more often the circumstances will make a difference. Just because your co-worker was awarded joint custody, you cannot assume you will be awarded joint custody. There are usually other circumstances your co-worker does not tell you about, and possibly does not understand.

Half of the People "Lose"

The legal system is designed to produce a winner and a loser, which usually precludes a "win-win" situation that might be possible (and more fair) with some other type of system. Remember, there are two sides to every legal issue, and there is only one winner. Do not expect to have every detail go your way. If you leave anything to the judge to decide, you can expect to have some things go the opposing party's way.

THE PARTICIPANTS

Since the law and the legal system are often compared to a game, just like games, it is important to know the players:

The Judge

The judge has the power to decide the legal issues in your case and whether you are entitled to whatever it is you went to court to receive. The judge is the last person you want to make angry! Judges have large caseloads, and they like it best when your case can be concluded quickly and without hassle. The more you and the opposing party can agree upon and the more complete your paperwork is, the more you will please the judge.

The Judge's Secretary

The judge's secretary sets the hearings for the judge, and can frequently answer many of your questions about the procedure and what the judge would like or requires. Once again, you do not want to make an enemy of the secretary. This means that you do not call often, and do not ask too many questions. A few questions are okay, and you might want to start off saying that you just want to make sure you have everything in order for the judge. Be friendly and courteous, even if the secretary is rude. The secretary has a large caseload just like the judge, and might be suffering from stress, or he or she might just be a nasty person. You will get farther by being pleasant than by arguing or complaining.

The Court Clerk

While the secretary usually only works for one judge, the court clerk works with all of the judges. The clerk's office is the central place where all of the court files are kept. The clerk files your court papers and keeps the official records of your court action. Most people who work in the clerk's office are friendly and helpful. While they cannot give you legal advice (such as telling you what to say in your court papers), they can help explain the system and the procedures (such as telling you what type of papers must be filed). The clerk has the power to accept or reject your papers, so you want to stay on their good side. If the clerk tells you to change something in your papers, just change it. Do not argue or complain.

Lawyers

Lawyers serve as guides through the legal system, and as modern-day hired guns. They try to guide their own client, while trying to confuse, manipulate, or outmaneuver their opponent. Chapter 3 discusses lawyers in more detail.

THE LAW IN YOUR STATE

Each state has its own laws and procedures, and there may be different procedures in various counties within a state. Therefore, a book such as this cannot possibly explain the details of the law and procedure of every court in the country. However, Appendix A of this book will be a good starting point. This will tell you the title of the set of books containing the law of your state, how the courts and the parties are designated on legal papers, and give you a summary of the factors the court in your state will use to make determinations on the matters of child custody, child support, and the termination of parental rights.

To obtain more information, call or visit the clerk of the court where you will be filing your case. The clerk will be able to tell you if there are any required forms you will need, how much filing fees are, where the nearest law library is located, and may give you limited guidance through the court procedures. The clerk may also provide forms for you to use. Such forms may be given out for free, or there may be a small charge for them. Court clerks cannot give you legal advice, however, as this would constitute practicing law without a license. The amount of assistance you will obtain from a clerk will vary from court to court, from no assistance at all to a lot of valuable help.

It is also strongly suggested that you visit a law library. These are usually located in, or near, the courthouse. Law libraries may also be found at law schools. Law libraries may have limitations on who may use them (for example, county law libraries may only be open to members of the bar, and law school libraries may only be open to students and faculty), or the times when they may be open to the general public may be limited. However, in most locations, county law libraries and state-supported law schools will be available to you. The next section of this chapter will help you find what you need at the law library.

LEGAL RESEARCH

To be certain you are doing things correctly, you might need to do a little research. Appendix A will provide a starting point.

After reading this book, you may want to visit a local law library. One can usually be found in or near your county courthouse. If you live near a law school, you can also find a law library there. The public library might also have copies of your state statutes or code. Some typical legal sources are discussed below.

> # PARENT TIP
>
> ---
>
> Do not hesitate to ask a librarian to help you find what you need. A librarian cannot give you legal advice, but can show you where to find your state's laws and other books on the type of case you are filing.

Statutes or Code

The main source of information will be the set of volumes that contains the laws passed by your state legislature. Depending upon your state, these will be referred to as either the statutes or the code of your state. (For example, the North Carolina General Statutes or the Mississippi Code). Appendix A includes the title of the set of laws for each state. Ask the law librarian for help if you have any problems locating your state's statutes or code. Each year the state legislatures meet and change the law; therefore, it is important to be sure you have the most current version.

Practice Manuals

At the law library, you will also be able to find books containing detailed information about the laws in your state, some of which may include sample forms. Some of these books are written in connection with continuing education seminars for lawyers. They can be very helpful in answering your questions about specific situations.

Court Rules

Court rules or procedures are those that are applied in the courts of your state. They might also contain some approved forms. You probably will not need to use the court rules, but they might be helpful if the court clerk or judge tells you that you have not done something right. In such a case, you might need to read the rule to find out how to correct the problem.

You probably will not need to do anymore research than to look up the law provisions in your state's statutes or code and look at some forms in a form or procedure book. However, just in case you need (or want) to go farther with your research, some information to help you is provided below. In addition to the laws passed by the legislature, law is also made by the decisions of the judges in various cases each year. To find this case law, you will need to go to a law library. In addition to annotated codes or statutes, there are several types of books used to find case law.

Digests

A digest is a set of volumes that give short summaries of appeals court cases and directs you to where you can find the court's full written opinion. The information in the digest is arranged alphabetically by subject. Locate the digest for your state (such as *New York Digest*). Look in the index to find the chapter to which you should refer.

Case Reporters

Case reporters are where the appeals courts publish their written opinions on the cases they hear. There might be a specific reporter for your state, or you might need to use a regional reporter that contains cases from several states in your area. There might be two series of the regional reporter, the second series being newer than the first. For example, if the digest tells you that the case of *Smith v. Smith* is located at 149 So.2d 721, you can find the case by going to Volume 149 of the *Southern Reporter 2d Series*, and turning to page 721. In its opinion, the court will discuss what the case was about, what questions of law were presented for consideration, and what the court decided and why.

Legal Encyclopedia

A legal encyclopedia is similar to a regular encyclopedia. You simply look up the subject you want, such as "paternity," and it gives you a summary of the law on that subject. It will also refer you to specific court cases which can then be found in the reporter. On a national level, the two main sets of legal encyclopedias are *American Jurisprudence* (Am. Jur.) and *Corpus Juris Secundum* (C.J.S.). You might also find a set for your state, such as the *Texas Jurisprudence.*

–3–
HIRING AN ATTORNEY

Whether you need an attorney will depend upon many factors, such as how comfortable you feel handling the matter yourself, whether your situation is more complicated than usual, and how much opposition you get from the opposing party or the opposing party's attorney. It might also be advisable to hire an attorney if you encounter a judge with a hostile attitude.

DO YOU WANT A LAWYER?

One of the first questions you will want to consider, and most likely one of the reasons you are reading this book, is to answer the question: How much will an attorney cost?

Attorneys come in all ages, shapes, sizes, sexes, racial, and ethnic groups—

PARENT TIP

A very general rule is that you should consider hiring an attorney whenever you reach a point where you no longer feel comfortable representing yourself. This point will vary greatly with each person, so there is no easier way to be more definite.

and price ranges. Lawyers usually charge an hourly rate ranging from about $75 to $300 per hour. Of course, these fees vary from state-to-state. Most new attorneys are less expensive and are quite capable of handling simple matters. However, if your situation is complicated, you may feel more comfortable with a more experienced lawyer.

Another question many people have is: Can I get a court appointed lawyer? A court appointed lawyer is a lawyer the judge appoints to represent a party in a court action. Generally, the court will only appoint a lawyer to represent people who have been charged with a crime and who cannot afford an attorney. However, in some states, the court may also appoint an attorney to represent people in the following situations:

- ♦ a parent who is subject to having their parental rights terminated;
- ♦ a man who has been served with a paternity action; or,
- ♦ a man facing criminal charges relating to the failure to pay child support.

It is important to note that a court appointed lawyer is not necessarily free. You may be responsible for reimbursing the state for the cost of the attorney. However, you can expect the fee will be less than what you would pay for hiring an attorney on your own.

Advantages to Hiring a Lawyer

Following are some of the advantages to hiring a lawyer.

- ♦ Judges and other attorneys might take you more seriously. Most judges prefer both parties to have attorneys. They feel this helps the case move in a more orderly fashion because both sides will know the procedures and relevant issues. Persons representing themselves very often waste much time on matters that have absolutely no bearing on the outcome of the case.
- ♦ A lawyer will serve as a "buffer" between you and the opposing party, which can lead to a quicker passage through the legal system by reducing the chance for emotions to take control and confuse issues.
- ♦ Attorneys prefer to deal with other attorneys for the same reasons judges prefer both parties have lawyers. However, if you become familiar with this book and conduct yourself in a calm and proper manner, you should have no trouble.
- ♦ You can let your attorney worry about all of the details. By having an attorney, you only need to become generally familiar with the contents of this book. It will be your attorney's job to

file the proper papers in the correct form and to deal with the clerks, the judge, the sheriff, the opposing party, and the opposing party's attorney.

◆ Lawyers provide professional assistance with problems. It is an advantage to have an attorney in the event your case is complicated, or suddenly becomes complicated. It can also be comforting to have a lawyer to turn to for advice and to answer questions.

Advantages to Representing Yourself

The following are some advantages to representing yourself.

◆ You save the cost of retaining a lawyer.

◆ Sometimes judges feel more sympathetic toward a person not represented by an attorney, resulting in the unrepresented person being allowed a certain amount of leeway with the rules.

◆ The procedure might be faster. Two of the most frequent complaints about lawyers received by the bar association involve delays in completing the case and the failure to return phone calls. Most lawyers have a heavy caseload, which sometimes results in cases being neglected for lengthy periods of time. If you are following the progress of your own case, you will be able to diligently push it through the system.

◆ Selecting an attorney is not easy. As the next section shows, it is hard to know whether you are selecting an attorney with whom you will be comfortable.

Middle Ground

You may want to look for an attorney who is willing to accept an hourly fee to answer your questions and give you help when you need assistance. This will save you some legal costs but still allow you to obtain some professional advice. Just be aware that lawyers often find fault with anything they did not personally prepare. A lawyer might tell you that you have done everything wrong and try to persuade you to have him handle your case entirely. So you might want to see a lawyer only if you have encountered a problem at the clerk's office or with the judge.

SELECTING AN ATTORNEY

This is a two-step process. First you need to decide which attorney to make an appointment with, then you need to decide if you want to hire that attorney.

Finding Lawyers

The following are some suggestions to help you locate lawyers for further consideration.

- Ask a friend. A common, and frequently the best way to find a lawyer is to ask someone you know to recommend one. This is especially helpful if the lawyer represented your friend in a similar matter.
- Attorney referral service. You can find one by looking in the yellow pages phone directory under "Attorney Referral Service" or "Attorneys." This service is usually provided by the state or county bar association, and is designed to match a client with an attorney handling cases in the area of law the client needs. The referral service does not guarantee the quality of work nor the level of experience or ability of the attorney. Finding a lawyer this way will at least connect you with one who is interested in family law matters and who probably has some experience in that area.
- Yellow pages. Check under the heading "Attorneys" in the yellow pages phone directory. Many of the lawyers and law firms will place display ads here indicating their areas of practice and educational backgrounds. Look for ads for firms or lawyers that indicate they practice "family law" or "domestic relations."
- Ask another lawyer. If you have used the services of an attorney in the past for some other matter (for example, a real estate closing, traffic ticket, or will), you might want to ask her if she handles family law matters or could refer you to an attorney whose ability in the area of family law is respected.

Evaluating a Lawyer

Select three to five attorneys worthy of further consideration. Call each attorney's office, explain that you are interested in seeking assistance, and ask the following the questions:

- Does the attorney (or firm) handle the type of case in which you are involved?
- How much can you expect it to cost?
- How soon can you get an appointment?

If you like the answers you get, ask if you can speak to the attorney. Some offices will permit this, but others will require you to make an appointment. Make the appointment if that is what is required. Once you get in contact with the attorney (either on the phone or at the appointment), ask the following questions:

- How much will it cost?
- How will the fee be paid?
- How long has the attorney been in practice?
- How long has the attorney been in practice in your state?
- What percentage of the attorney's cases involve family law matters? (Do not expect an exact answer, but you should get a rough estimate that is at least twenty percent.)
- How long will it take? (Again, do not expect an exact answer, but the attorney should be able to give you an average range and discuss things that might make a difference.)

If you get acceptable answers to these questions, it is time to ask yourself the following questions about the lawyer:

- Do you feel comfortable talking to the lawyer?
- Is the lawyer friendly toward you?
- Does the lawyer seem confident in himself or herself?
- Does the lawyer seem to be straightforward with you and able to explain things so you understand?

If you get satisfactory answers to all of these questions you probably have a lawyer with whom you will be able to work. Most clients are happiest with an attorney with whom they feel comfortable.

WORKING WITH AN ATTORNEY

You will work best with your attorney if you keep an open, honest, and friendly attitude. Also consider the following suggestions.

Ask Questions

If you want to know something or if you do not understand something, ask your attorney. If you do not understand the answer, ask your lawyer to explain it again. There are many points of law that even lawyers do not fully understand, so do not be embarrassed to ask questions. Many people who say they had a bad experience with a lawyer either did not ask enough questions or had a lawyer who would not take the time to explain things to them. If your lawyer is not taking the time to explain what he is doing, it might be time to look for a new lawyer.

Complete Information

Give your lawyer complete information. Anything you tell your attorney is confidential. An attorney can lose his license to practice if he reveals information without your permission. So do not hold back. Tell your lawyer everything, even if it does not seem important to you. There are many things that seem unimportant to people who are not lawyers which can change the outcome of a case. Do not keep something back because you are afraid it will hurt your case. It will definitely do that if your lawyer does not find out about it until he hears it in court from the opposing party's attorney. If he knows in advance, he can plan to eliminate or reduce the damage to your case.

Accept Reality

Listen to what your lawyer tells you about the law and the system and accept it. It will do you no good to argue because the law or the system does not work the way you think it should. For example, if your lawyer tells you that the judge cannot hear your case for two weeks, do not try demanding that he set a hearing tomorrow. By refusing to accept reality, you are only setting yourself up for disappointment. (Keep in mind that it is not your attorney's fault that the system is not perfect, or that the law does not say what you would like it to say.)

Patience

Be patient. This applies to your dealings with the system (which is often slow, as we discussed earlier) as well as with your attorney. Do not expect your lawyer to return your phone call within an hour. He might not be able to return it the same day either. Most lawyers are very busy and overworked. It is rare that an attorney can maintain a full caseload and still make each client feel as if he is the only client.

The Lawyer's Secretary

Talk to your lawyer's secretary. He or she can be a valuable source of information. Be friendly and get to know him. Often the secretary will be able to answer your questions, and you will not get a bill for the time you talk to him or her. Many lawyers also have a *legal assistant* or *paralegal* who may be able to answer your questions. However, some lawyers bill their clients for a paralegal's time, although at a lower hourly rate than is billed for the attorney's time. At the time you hire your attorney, he or she should inform you of such charges.

Dealing with the Opposing Party

Let your attorney deal with the opposing party. It is your lawyer's job to communicate with the opposing party or the opposing party's lawyer. Allow your lawyer do his or her job. Many lawyers have had clients lose or damage their case when the client decided to say or do something on their own.

Promptness

Be on time for appointments with your lawyer and for court hearings. Especially for a court hearing, it is a good idea to arrive early.

Keep Your Case Moving

Many lawyers operate on the old principle of the "squeaking wheel gets the oil." Work on a case tends to get put off until a deadline is near, an emergency develops, or the client calls. This happens because many lawyers take more cases than can be effectively handled in order to increase their income. Your task is to become a "squeaking wheel" that does not squeak too much. Whenever you talk to your lawyer ask the following questions.

- ◆ What is the next step?
- ◆ When do you expect it to be done?
- ◆ When should I talk to you next?

If you do not hear from the lawyer when you expect to, call her/him the following day. Do not remind your lawyer that he/she did not call; just ask how things are going.

Saving Money

Of course you do not want to spend unnecessary money for an attorney. Here are a few things you can do to avoid excess legal fees.

- ◆ Do not make unnecessary phone calls to your lawyer.
- ◆ Give information to the secretary whenever possible.
- ◆ Direct your questions to the secretary first, who will refer it to the attorney if he or she cannot answer it.
- ◆ Plan your phone calls so you can get to the point and take less of your attorney's time.
- ◆ Do some legwork yourself. Pick up and deliver papers, for example. Ask your attorney what you can do to assist with your case.
- ◆ Be prepared for appointments. Plan your visits—make an outline of what you want to discuss and what question you want to ask, get to the point, and have all related papers with you.

Paying Your Bill

No client gets prompt attention like a client who pays his lawyer on time. However, you are entitled to an itemized bill, showing what the attorney did and how much time it took. Many attorneys will have you sign an agreement that states how you will be charged, what is included in the hourly fee, and what is extra. Review your bill carefully.

Firing Your Lawyer

If you find that you can no longer work with your lawyer, or do not trust your lawyer, it is time to go it alone or to get a new attorney. You will need to send your lawyer a letter stating that you no longer desire his or her services and are discharging him or her from your case. Also, state that you will be coming by his or her office the following day to pick up your file. If he or she refuses to give out your file, for any reason, contact your state's bar association about filing a complaint or grievance against the lawyer. Of course, you will need to settle any remaining fees charged.

−4−

COURT PROCEDURES

If you decide to hire an attorney, then he or she will perform the next three steps in the process:

> (1) preparing the legal forms;
> (2) filing the forms with the court clerk, and,
> (3) notifying the opposing party.

However, if you decide *not* to hire an attorney, then you can enforce your rights by representing yourself. You will need to initiate the legal action by preparing and filing the necessary legal forms.

LEGAL FORMS

There is nothing magical about legal forms. They are simply a way of communicating information to the court. Appendix B contains various sample forms for you to use. The forms you use most meet the requirements of your court.

> ## PARENT TIP
>
> Visit the court clerk's office. Tell the clerk that you would like to see a file of the type of case you are filing. These files are usually open to the public, and you should be allowed to look at one. You will want to copy the format of the papers in these files as closely as possible.

Case Style

Legal forms begin with the identification of the court and the names of the parties. This part of the form is called the *caption* or *case style*. Once your case is assigned a case number by the court clerk, the case number will also become part of the case style. The information for your state in Appendix A will help you determine the proper case style. This will include how the court and the parties are designated. You should also look at how case styles have been set up in the files you review at the court clerk's office. Below is an example of a case style for a fictional state:

STATE OF SUPERIOR
IN THE CIRCUIT COURT OF THE FOURTH JUDICIAL CIRCUIT,
IN AND FOR MONROE COUNTY

_____Timothy Jones_____,

                           Petitioner,   Custody Complaint

                                            Case No. _____

and

_____Jacqueline Jones_____,

                           Respondent.

The case style will vary, depending upon the state in which you live. The title of the court will be different in each state. For example, in California the court will be "Superior Court of California, County of _____" (you will need to fill in the name of the county where you are filing your case). Some states just list the name of the county; others have the state geographically divided into numbered circuits or divisions. The listing for your state in Appendix A will tell you how the courts are designated in your state.

Any blank spaces will need to be filled in with the proper county or judicial circuit number (or both). If the circuit number needs to be filled in, it will often be written out instead of using a numeral (e.g., "Fourth," not "4th"). A few states also call the courts by a different name in various counties. Do not forget to go to the clerk's office and ask to see the file of someone else. Look in the file, notice how the case style is arranged, then use the same format in your papers. If you have any questions about the proper case style, ask the court clerk. Case styles are usually established by court rules.

Different states also refer to the parties in various ways. The parties are the people involved in the case. The two most common ways of referring to the parties in a case are as the plaintiff and defendant and the petitioner and respondent. Again, do not forget to look at someone else's file at the court clerk's office.

Typing is preferred by judges, and gives a much more professional appearance than handwriting, but it may not be absolutely necessary for you use a typewriter to fill in the forms. If you do not own a typewriter, borrow one from a friend, rent one for a day, or ask if one is available at your local library or court clerk's office. If typing is not possible, ask the court clerk if forms filled in by hand will be accepted. If so, print the information and be sure that your writing can be easily read.

THE COMPLAINT OR PETITION

The basic paper you file to begin the legal process is called a *complaint* or *petition*, depending upon the state and the type of case. The title may vary from state to state for a particular type of case. For example, one state may call it a *complaint for paternity*, another state may call it a *petition for paternity*, and still another state may call it a *petition to establish paternity*.

Even within a state, the title may vary depending upon the type of case. For example, you may file a complaint in a paternity case (*complaint for paternity*), but a petition in a custody case (*petition for custody*). In this book, the words complaint and petition will be used interchangeably; however, be sure to use the correct name used in your state for the type of case you will file.

Appendix B includes sample complaints for:

◆ paternity;
◆ custody;
◆ visitation;
◆ child support; and,
◆ termination of parental rights.

More specific information about each type of complaint is given in the chapter about that particular type of case. The following is general information that is usually applicable to any type of complaint.

A complaint identifies the court and the parties, states the facts that one party claims entitle him or her to some type of judgment, and asks the court to grant that judgment.

Identifying the court and the parties is the purpose of the case style, which was discussed earlier in this chapter. The person who is filing the case is called either the *plaintiff* (or sometimes the *complainant*) in a complaint, and is called the *petitioner* in a petition. The person who is being sued is usually called the *defendant* in a complaint and the *respondent* in a petition.

What information is required to be in the main body of the complaint is usually set forth in the state's statutes or code. This information will vary depending upon the type of case. For example, the statute relating to paternity cases will state what information must be included in a complaint for paternity, and the custody statutes will tell what information must be in a complaint for custody.

SUMMONS

A *Summons* is a legal document that is required to be delivered (along with the complaint) to the person being sued. The purpose of the summons is to make it clear to the person being sued that he or she has certain obligations and rights. In all states, the summons advises the person that he or she is being sued, that he or she must file some kind of response to the complaint within a certain number of days, and that if a response is not filed he or she may lose the case by default. The summons may also be written in two or more languages, and may contain other obligations and rights.

Each state, and sometimes each county or court subdivision within a state, has its own official summons form. These official forms are usually available from the court clerk, and it is required that you use the official form. An example of a *Summons* may be found as form I in Appendix B of this book. Most states have very specific requirements for their summons forms, so be sure to comply with your state's requirements.

SUPPORTING DOCUMENTS

Some states require certain documents to be filed along with the complaint. The following are examples of some of the supporting documents you may need.

Verification

The *Verification* is usually attached to the complaint. A *verification* is a document which you sign before a notary public. In this sworn statement you declare that all of the information included in the complaint is true, either because you know first-hand that it is true or because you believe it to be true. This makes your complaint a statement under oath, subjecting you to being charged with perjury if you knowingly make a false statement in your complaint. See the sample *Verification* (form F) in Appendix B.

Uniform Child Custody Jurisdiction Act Affidavit

The *Uniform Child Custody Jurisdiction Act Affidavit* is either attached to, or filed along with, a custody or visitation complaint. This form came to be as the result of people moving from state to state to try to get a favorable custody order. The purpose of this form is to alert the court if there is a possible conflict with either a court proceeding in another state, or in another court in the same state.

In some states, the information in this form may be put directly into the complaint instead of filing a separate form. This form requires some basic information about where, and with whom, the child has lived for the past few years; and whether there are, or have been, any other court proceedings that might affect custody or visitation (such as a case for custody, visitation, abuse, neglect, termination of parental rights, etc.). See the sample *Uniform Child Custody Act Affidavit* (form G) in Appendix B.

Cover Sheet

A *cover sheet* is a general term for various administrative forms that many states require to be filed with a complaint. It may be called a cover sheet or by some other name. The purpose of a *cover sheet* is to help the court keep track of how many cases it handles each year, how many of each type of case it handles, and other statistical information. Cover sheets are usually available from the court clerk and can be filled out at the time you go to file your case. An example of a typical cover sheet is included as form N in Appendix B.

Financial Affidavit

A *Financial Affidavit* will usually be required in cases involving child support. Both parties will be required to file their own *Financial Affidavit*, which will include information about their income, expenses, what they own, and what they owe. This information will serve as a basis for calculating the amount of child support. *Financial Affidavits* are often required in custody cases also, either to satisfy the court that the person seeking custody will be able to support the child, or because the question of child support is also raised in the case. Some states have an official form for this purpose, and others leave it up to the parties to come up with their own form.

Birth Certificate

Depending upon the type of case you are filing, and the state in which you file, you may be required to file a certified copy of the child's birth certificate.

There are numerous other forms that may be required by your court, and it is impossible to list them all here. To find out what other forms you may need you can ask the court clerk, go to the clerk's office and look at a file for the same type of case you are filing, or do some research at the nearest law library.

FILING WITH THE COURT CLERK

Once your initial documents are prepared, you will need to file your case with the court clerk. First, make at least *three copies* of your complaint and any other papers you have prepared. This will give you one copy to file with the clerk, one for the opposing party, one for yourself and one extra copy just in case the clerk asks for two copies, or you decide to hire an attorney and need a copy for him or her. In some states there may be another government office that must receive a copy.

Filing is about as simple as making a bank deposit, although the following information will help things go more smoothly. Call the court clerk's office. You can probably find the phone number under the county government section of your phone directory. Ask the clerk the following questions (along with any other questions that come to mind, such as where the clerk's office is located and what their hours are):

- How much is the filing fee for the type of case you plan to file?
- Does the court have any special forms that need to be filed with the complaint and where can you obtain them?
- How many copies of the complaint and other forms do you need to file with the clerk?

Next, take your complaint and any other papers to be filed to the clerk's office. The clerk handles many different types of cases, so be sure to look for signs telling you to which office or window to go. You should be looking for signs that say such things as "Family Court," "Family Division," "Filing," etc. If it is too confusing, ask someone where you file your type of case.

Once you have found the right place, simply hand the papers to the clerk and say, "I would like to file this." The clerk will examine the papers, then do one of two things: either say, "Thank you" (and collect the filing fee or direct you where to pay it), or tell you that something is not correct. If you are told something is wrong, ask the clerk to explain to you what is wrong and how to correct the problem. Although clerks are not permitted to give legal advice, the types of problems they spot are usually minor things that they can tell you how to correct. Often it is possible to figure out how to correct it from the way the clerk explains what is wrong.

NOTIFYING NECESSARY PARTIES

In all lawsuits, there are certain people who must be officially notified. In all cases, you will need to notify the other parent. Depending upon the type of case and the state, you may also need to notify certain state agencies, such as the prosecutor's office or the social service agency. If someone other than you or the other parent is the legal custodian or guardian of the child, that person must also be notified.

The most common way to notify the opposing party that you filed a lawsuit against them is called *personal service*. This is where the sheriff, or someone else designated by the judge, personally delivers the papers to the other person.

Usually, the initial papers that must be delivered are the *Complaint* and the *Summons*. The complaint tells the other person what the lawsuit is about (paternity, custody, etc.), and the *Summons* gives the person his or her legal rights and obligations (most importantly, that they have a certain number of days in which to formally respond to the complaint).

Be sure to check with the court clerk about the proper form for the *Summons* because this varies for each state and possibly even for each county. Often, the clerk will provide you with the official *Summons* form. An example of a typical *Summons* is found in Appendix B (see form I), but you will need to use the form for your state and county. If the clerk cannot provide you with the *Summons* form, there are two sources you can use to find one:

(1) you can check at your local law library; or

(2) you can look at a file for someone else's case at the clerk's office.

In most cases, the files of lawsuits are open to the general public. Just be sure you look at a file for the same type of case you are filing (e.g., custody, child support, paternity, termination of parental rights, etc.) because the form of the *Summons* may be different in each type of case.

Once you have prepared the *Summons*, take it to the clerk for signature. Then, call the county sheriff's office in the county where the opposing party lives, and ask how much it will cost to have him or her served with the papers, and how many copies of the *Complaint* and *Summons* need to be provided to the sheriff's office. Deliver or mail the required copies of your *Summons* and *Complaint* (together with any other papers you filed), and a check or money order for the service fee to the sheriff's office.

A sheriff's deputy will personally deliver the papers to the opposing party. Of course, you must give the sheriff accurate information about where the person can be found. If there are several addresses where the person to be served might be found (such as home, a relative's, and work), enclose a letter to the sheriff with all of the addresses and any other information that may help the sheriff find the person (such as the hours the opposing party works).

Be sure to give the sheriff information that will be truly useful to get the opposing party served, and do not just speculate where he or she might be. The deputy will fill out a form to verify that the papers were delivered (including the date and time they were delivered), and will file a copy of that form with the court clerk. The deputy should also send you a copy to let you know the opposing party has been served, but you may need to check your court file in the clerk's office.

The Other Party's Response

Once the other person has been served, he or she has a certain number of days in which to formally respond. In most states, this will be between twenty and thirty days. Read your state's summons form to find out how many days apply to your case. The person can respond in several ways. He or she may file a paper with the court, which is usually called an *Answer* or a *Response*. (See form H in Appendix B for a sample of the form.) Such a paper either admits or denies the statements in your complaint or petition. Instead, the other person may file one of several types of *Motions* (such a *Motion to Dismiss* or *Motion for Summary Judgment*), which will raise some issue that must be decided before he or she will be required to file an answer or response.

Other Notices

Once you know the date the opposing party was served, you can count the number of days to find out when their response is due. Wait an additional five days to allow for mailing and clerk's office filing delay, then go to the clerk's office and see if any kind of response is in your court file. If no response has been filed, you will proceed to seek a default, which is discussed in more detail later in this chapter.

Once the opposing party has been served with the *Summons* and *Complaint* and that party has filed an *Answer* or response, you may simply mail him or her copies of any papers you file later. All you need to do is sign a statement, called a *Certificate of Service*, that you mailed copies to the opposing party. Some of the forms will have a *Certificate of Service* for you to complete. If any form you file does not contain one, you will need to complete a *Certificate of Service*. For a sample completed *Certificate of Service*, see form J in Appendix B.

Once you get a hearing date set with the judge, you will need to notify the opposing party of when the hearing will be. This is discussed in Chapter 5.

If You Cannot Locate the Other Party

There is a way to formally notify the opposing party by publishing a notice in the newspaper if you cannot locate him/her yourself. However, it can be complicated and may require the assistance of an attorney. Unfortunately, you may not be able to accomplish certain things unless the opposing party is present. For example, if you want visitation or custody, you will need to be able to locate the person who has custody of the child in order to do so. It will also be difficult to establish paternity if the opposing party cannot be located in order to submit to a scientific paternity test.

In most states, the procedure for service by publication involves the following four steps:

- ◆ conducting a search to try to locate the missing party;
- ◆ filing a motion with the court, telling the judge what you have done to try to find the missing party, and asking the judge to permit you to serve the other party by publication;
- ◆ having the required legal notice published in the appropriate newspaper, in the manner required by the law in your state; and,
- ◆ filing some kind of notice with the court to verify that the proper publication has taken place. (This will often be an affidavit from an employee of the newspaper, and may also involve filing a photocopy of the notice as it appeared in the newspaper.)

A word of caution before you decide to notify the opposing party by publication—if the procedures required in your state for service by publication are not strictly and carefully followed, then whatever the judge decides can be set aside at a later date.

For example, Jan filed an action to terminate her ex-husband's parental rights so that her new husband could adopt her child. She had not seen her ex-husband in five years and had no idea where he lived. She decided to serve him by publication. Jan failed to follow the proper procedure with respect to how long the notice should run in the newspaper. Both the judge and the clerk overlooked the error. At the trial, the judge ruled in Jan's favor and terminated her ex-husband's parental rights. Three years later, after the child was adopted, Jan's ex-husband showed up and wanted to visit with the child. In this situation, the ex-husband would have grounds to challenge the termination, since he was not properly served with notice of the lawsuit.

What is the moral of this story? Although there are sample forms in the appendix of this book, you should not attempt to serve the opposing party by publication until you are well acquainted with the laws in your state.

First, you need to conduct what is called a *diligent search* for the missing party. This does not require you to hire a private investigator; however, at a minimum you will be expected to do the following.

- Contact the missing party's relatives, friends, and acquaintances.
- Check with the post office where the missing party last lived to see if a forwarding address request was filed.
- Look in the telephone book and call directory assistance in the area where the missing party last lived, or may now live.
- Contact the appropriate state agencies in the state where the missing party last lived, or may now live, to see if he or she has a driver's license or car registration there.
- Follow through on any other contacts. For example, if you know the missing party was in the military, you should contact the base or post where he or she was last stationed.

Once your diligent search has been conducted (and you have not located him or her), you should determine the following.

◆ What newspapers are qualified to publish legal notices? Most states have requirements for the type of newspaper that can be used for publishing a legal notice. Placing a legal notice in many major daily newspapers can be very expensive. Many communities have smaller newspapers, which meet the state requirements and offer much cheaper rates.

◆ How many times, and over what period of time, must the notice appear in the newspaper?

◆ Where must the notice be published? Most states require you to publish the notice in the city or town where the opposing party was last seen or last resided.

◆ What information must be included in the notice?

To find out this information, as well as what forms to use and what procedures to follow, you may:

◆ Ask the clerk of the court if any standardized forms for service by publication are available. These forms will often include instructions.

◆ Refer to your state's court rules, or code or statutes. Start with the index under "service by publication."

◆ Ask a law librarian to refer you to any form books that might contain this information.

◆ Contact an attorney to schedule a consultation about how to serve someone by publication.

IF THE OTHER PARENT FILED AGAINST YOU

If you are the one being served with a *Complaint* and *Summons*, you will need to file an *Answer*. This is also called a *Response* in some states. The papers will include how many days you have in which to file your answer. This time period is usually twenty days in most states, but may be longer in others. Do not let this time period pass. For a sample completed *Answer*, see form H in Appendix B.

–5–

COURT HEARINGS

SCHEDULING COURT HEARINGS

You will need to set a hearing date for the final hearing, or for any preliminary matters that require a hearing. To obtain a court date, you will need to contact either the court clerk or the judge's secretary, depending upon the practice in your county. (If you do not know which judge, call the court clerk, give the clerk your case number, and ask for the name and phone number of the judge assigned to your case.) You can then either call or go see that judge's secretary and tell him or her you would like to set a final hearing date for whatever type case you filed. Usually the judge's phone number can be found in the government section of your phone book.

Notifying Necessary Parties

Once you get a hearing date set with the judge, you will need to notify the opposing party of when the hearing will be. This is done by preparing a *Notice of Hearing*.

First, check with the court clerk to see if they have an official form. If not, look at a case file at the clerk's office, or check your local law library for the *Notice of Hearing* forms used in your state or county. You will need four copies of the *Notice of Hearing*. Mail one to the opposing party, file the original with the court clerk, and keep two copies for yourself.

PREPARING YOUR CASE

To prepare for the hearing, you need to decide what you are going to say, what documents and witnesses (if any) you will present, and the order in which you will present them. You should make a list of each fact you intend to prove, and next to each fact write down how you will prove it. For example:

- ◆ your contact with the child—phone records and copies of letters you have mailed;
- ◆ your current income—tax returns and pay stubs; and,
- ◆ your relationship with the opposing party—photographs of you and the opposing party, or a copy of an apartment lease agreement with both of your names.

PARENT TIP

Have your notes ready to keep you on track at the hearing. Be sure to have your documents arranged in the order you will present them. If you have witnesses, prepare a set of your written questions for each witness. Arrange the sets of question in the order in which you will have the witnesses testify.

WITNESSES

Selecting and interviewing witnesses is one of the most important aspects of preparing for the hearing. The witnesses you choose to testify for you will depend upon what you are trying to prove at the hearing. For child custody and visitation issues, witnesses may include relatives, friends, neighbors, police officers, child abuse investigators, social workers, doctors, psychologists, your child's school counselors, and teachers. For financial issues in child support cases, witnesses may include employers, bank officials, appraisers, friends, neighbors, and relatives who can verify your financial situation and that of the opposing party.

You will need to decide who you think would be a good witness to help your position. First, make a list of each fact you want to prove at the hearing. Again, this will depend upon the issues in dispute. Beside each fact, write down the name of the witness or witnesses you believe will be able to testify to that fact. Next, make a list of each potential witness, their address and telephone number, what fact they will prove for you, and what you expect each will say in court.

Your next step is to talk to each potential witness to be sure of what they would say at the hearing. Never assume what a witness will say at the hearing; find out for sure by interviewing them. Many cases have been lost by a witness giving surprise testimony at a hearing. One of the first lessons law students are taught about questioning witnesses at a hearing is: "Never ask a question unless you know what the answer will be."

For each witness you interview, you want to ask specific questions that you might ask at the hearing, and allow the witness to describe what he or she saw, heard, and "knows." In addition to assuring yourself what the witness will say, this will allow you to find out new information and possibly lead you to other witnesses.

One alternative is to ask the witness to give you a written, signed statement of what they saw, heard, and know. Try to have someone with you when you interview the witness. That person can testify to the original statements in the event the witness changes his or her story at the hearing. The important message here is to be as sure as possible what your witnesses will say before you put them on the witness stand.

Expert Witnesses

Especially in custody and termination of parental rights cases, it may be necessary to have an *expert witness* testify. An expert witness testifies because of, and in relation to, his or her special education, training, or experience, such as a doctor or psychologist. At the hearing, it is first necessary to have the judge determine that the witness is qualified as an expert. This is usually done by asking the witness to tell about his or her profession and to describe his or her training and job experience.

Notifying Witnesses

The best way to notify witnesses of your hearing date is by having the sheriff serve them with a *Subpoena*. It is a good idea to call your witnesses to let them know of the hearing date, and that they will be receiving a subpoena. It is not absolutely necessary to serve a subpoena on a witness who is willing to come voluntarily and help you. But, if they have car trouble or are ill on the hearing date, the judge will probably not continue the hearing so that they can testify at a later date unless they were served with a subpoena. The subpoena will also enable your witness to get off work to come to the hearing.

For doctors, psychologists, school teachers, police officers, etc., it is absolutely necessary that you serve them with subpoenas. Also, in order to force someone to appear at the hearing and testify, you will need to have the person served with a subpoena by the sheriff or someone else approved by the court.

Subpoenas should be served at least five days before the hearing, but no earlier than about two weeks. If you just need the person to testify, use a subpoena form commonly used in your state or county. Ask the court clerk for a subpoena form. Since the subpoena must be issued or signed by the clerk, they may have a form for you to use. An example of a typical *Subpoena* is included in Appendix B as form L.

There are two types of subpoena. One is called a *subpoena ad testificatum*, or often simply *Subpoena*, which orders the witness to appear and give testimony. The other is called a *subpoena duces tecum*, which orders the person to appear, testify, and bring documents or other items. Therefore, if you want the person to bring documents or other items to be introduced as evidence (such as payroll or medical records), you will need to use a *subpoena duces tecum*.

Many states use a single form, which provides some means of designating the type of subpoena (such as checking a box or writing in the words "Duces Tecum"). You will need to be careful to accurately describe the documents or other items you want the person to bring. For example, if you want payroll records, be sure to use the full name of the person whose records you want, their social security number if possible, and include the date of the pay periods you wish produced. The more specific you are, the more likely you are to get the information you want, and the more likely the judge will be willing to sanction the witness for failing to bring what was requested.

PRESENTING YOUR CASE

There are certain *rules of procedure* that are used in a court. These are really the rules of good conduct, or good manners, and are designed to keep things orderly. Many of the rules are written down, although some are unwritten customs that have developed over many years. Following these suggestions will make the judge respect you for your maturity and professional manner, and possibly even make him forget for a moment that you are not a lawyer. It will also increase the likelihood that you get the things you request.

- ◆ Show respect for the judge.
- ◆ If the judge interrupts you, stop talking and listen.
- ◆ The judge can only listen to one person at a time, so do not ever interrupt the opposing party when it is his or her time to speak. You will be given your chance to speak and address the comments made by the opposing party after the other party has had his or her say.
- ◆ Direct your comments to the judge, not the opposing party.
- ◆ Talk only when it is your turn.
- ◆ Stay focused on the subject, and answer the judge's questions simply and to the point.
- ◆ Remain calm and try to maintain your composure.
- ◆ Show respect for the opposing party. If you do not respect them, act as if you do.

Your Presentation

The judge will know you do not have a lawyer, and he may help you through the hearing by asking you what he needs to know, or even by telling you what you need to do to present your case. When you first meet the judge, smile and say, "Good morning, your Honor," or "Good afternoon, your Honor." Then follow his lead. If he starts guiding you, or asking questions, just let him control the hearing.

Otherwise, be prepared to give a brief opening statement, telling the judge that this is a final hearing on a complaint for whatever type action you filed, whether you and the opposing party have reached any agreement, and what issues need to be decided by the judge.

Sample Opening Statement:

> Good morning, your Honor. My name is Jane Doe. I am the Plaintiff. On June 1, 1999, I filed a complaint seeking custody, and child support on behalf of my three-year-old son, John Deer Doe. The defendant is John's father. The defendant and I were never married. We lived together for several years, and separated when my son was six months old. My son has been living with me exclusively since that time.
>
> I plan to call three witnesses, all of whom are present in court. I believe that my case will take about two hours. Thank you.

The judge may stop you before you have the chance to complete your opening statement, and just ask you to present your proof or evidence. This is usually done to save time. If this happens, submit your proof (which may simply be financial statements filed by you and the opposing party). The judge will probably swear you in and tell you to proceed. What you do next will depend on what issues need to be decided. This is where you will call your witnesses and introduce documents as evidence, as discussed earlier in this chapter. See the chapter on the type of case you have (support, custody, etc.) for more information about the kind of evidence you will need.

Rules of Evidence

Although this book cannot make you a lawyer, you should be aware of a few basic rules of evidence.

Relevancy. The documents you present to the judge, and the questions you ask witnesses, should be related to the facts you need to prove. For example, if you are trying to establish paternity, the fact that the opposing party's mother became angry when you asked to see the child has no relevancy to the issue. You need to determine what information you need in order to prove the issue at hand and stick to that information.

Hearsay. Generally, a witness cannot testify to what someone else told him or her. For example, suppose you are trying to get custody due to physical abuse in the other parent's home, and your neighbor saw the other parent beat your child with an electric cord. You need the neighbor in court to testify to what she saw. You cannot have your cousin testify that the neighbor told him she saw the beating.

This can also apply to documents containing statements made by someone who is not in court to testify. There are numerous exceptions to the hearsay rule, and many lawyers and judges do not fully understand this area of law. One important exception is that you can use any statements your opposing party made to the person testifying.

Documents. Usually, documents must be introduced at the hearing by someone's testimony. You need someone (it can even be you) who can identify the paper, and say who prepared the paper, and how they know who prepared the paper. For example, to introduce documents you received from your opposing party's employer, you can testify as to how you got the documents (although it will be much safer to have the employer there to testify).

Below is an example of how a document is typically presented by a third party's testimony at a hearing. The document is first marked as an *exhibit*, either with a letter or a number (e.g., "Plaintiff's Exhibit 1" or "Respondent's Exhibit A"). This is to make it clear from then on to which document is being referred. Often, one side's exhibits are marked with numbers, and the other side's exhibits are marked with letters. This helps to avoid confusion.

Once the exhibit is given a designation, it is presented to the witness to identify. In this example, the witness is a friend of the defendant in a case to establish paternity, and the document is a letter the witness received in which the defendant stated he was the father.

Plaintiff   (speaking to judge): "May I have this marked as Plaintiff's Exhibit 1?" (At same time, the Plaintiff hands a copy of the document to the opposing party or attorney.)

Judge: "So designated." (How a document is actually marked as an exhibit will vary. In some courts you will be expected to mark it yourself. In other courts it will be marked by the court reporter, judge's clerk, or some other court administrative employee in the courtroom. It may be marked by writing the exhibit number or letter on the document, or by affixing a sticker to it with the number or letter on the sticker.)

Plaintiff   (speaking to witness): "I am showing you what has been marked as Plaintiff's Exhibit 1. Can you identify this?"

Witness: "Yes."

Plaintiff: "What is it?"

Witness: "This is a letter I received from the defendant last April."

Plaintiff: "How do you know it is from the defendant?"

Witness: "I have known the defendant for ten years, and I am familiar with his handwriting. This letter is in the defendant's handwriting and the envelope it came in had his return address. Since I received it, the defendant has referred to it in conversations we have had."

Plaintiff   (to judge): "Your Honor, I move that Plaintiff's Exhibit 1 be admitted into evidence."

Judge: "So admitted." (Until this point, the exhibit is not officially a part of the evidence. What the Plaintiff has done so far is to show that the document is appropriate to become part of the evidence.)

Once the document has been properly marked, identified, and admitted into evidence, the plaintiff would ask the witness whatever questions are necessary to have the witness explain what information the document contains and show how it relates to the case.

Examining Witnesses

Examining a witness refers to asking questions of your witnesses (called *direct examination*), and of the opposing party's witnesses (called *cross-examination*). One problem most non-lawyers have with this is that they tend to start testifying instead of asking questions. This is not the time for you to explain anything.

You should be particularly careful in cross-examining the opposing party's witnesses. If you are not very sure what their answer will be, do not ask. Do not feel that you must ask questions of each witness. Often it is best to let the witness go without further damaging your case.

In questioning witnesses at the hearing you want to show three basic things:

(1) who the witness is;

(2) what the witness knows; and,

(3) how the witness knows it.

If you are using an expert witness, you will need to ask the witness about his or her education, training, and employment history, then ask the judge to qualify the person as an expert in whatever area you need his or her testimony. For each witness you should make a list of the questions you will ask, what the answer will prove, and the expected answer to each question. Keep in mind that most judges try to finish hearings as quickly as possible, so you do not want your witnesses to get off the track of what they need to say to prove your case.

THE JUDGE'S DECISION AND FINAL ORDER

At the end of the hearing, the judge will announce his or her decision. There is no point arguing, as judges are not likely to change a decision once it is announced. If the case does not turn out as you had hoped, try to take comfort in the fact that you did your best. Also, because there are so many things that are beyond your control, there is no point in getting down on yourself when things do not go your way.

Whatever the judge decides will need to be written and included in a document called a *Judgment* or *Order*. In some instances the clerk or judge's secretary will be responsible for preparing the order, filing it, and sending copies to the parties. However, in most instances, the judge will direct one of the parties to prepare the order. If you are responsible for preparing the order, you will need to make a note of exactly what the judge orders. Go home and prepare the order as the judge instructed. You will then need to take the document back to the judge for his or her signature. You do not have to worry too much about making a mistake because the judge usually will not sign it until it is an accurate reflection of what was ordered.

Once you complete the *Order*, you will need to complete a *Certificate of Service*, attach it to the order, and deliver it to the clerk. Provide the clerk with at least two extra copies, along with a stamped envelope addressed to yourself and a stamped envelope addressed to the opposing party. Ask the clerk whether you should sign and date the *Certificate of Service*. (Sometimes the clerk will handle the mailing of the order after the judge signs it, in which case he or she may sign the *Certificate of Service*.)

–6–

ESTABLISHING PATERNITY

Establishing paternity is the process of determining who is a particular child's father. Paternity can be established by the mere relationship of the parents and the child, by the father admitting in an official manner that he is the father, or by a court proceeding.

PATERNITY LAW AND PROCEDURE
Where paternity is in dispute or uncertain, scientific tests can be done. The most common paternity test uses DNA (genetic traits) to determine whether a given man could be the biological father of a given child (tests are discussed later in this chapter). In most states, a paternity action is a civil lawsuit that a person files to ask a court to determine whether a given man could be the biological father of a given child.

Who Needs to Establish Paternity?
You will need to establish paternity if it is not already established and you either want to enforce your rights as a parent (i.e., to secure custody or visitation rights), or want to force the child's father to live up to his obligations as a parent (i.e., pay child support, medical expenses, etc.). The following are examples of scenarios that might give rise to a paternity action:

- ◆ a mother is certain of paternity, but the father refuses to accept responsibility;
- ◆ a man suspects the woman he has been dating is carrying his baby, or discovers that a woman he once dated gave birth a few months after their breakup;

- ◆ a mother has had multiple sex partners and is not certain which man is the father of her child;
- ◆ an unmarried couple wants to go through the legal formality of establishing paternity in order to ensure their child is legally protected and formally legitimated; or,
- ◆ a man has doubts about whether he is the father of a child, and wants to make certain before agreeing to pay child support.

Relationship to Custody and Visitation

It is not necessary to establish paternity before filing for custody or visitation, unless paternity becomes an issue. If you are the mother, you just file for custody (or visitation) without any request to establish paternity. If you are the father, and the mother is not disputing that you are the father, you just file for custody (or visitation) without any request to establish paternity. However, if there is a question regarding paternity, that will need to be legally established before a custody or visitation action can proceed. This almost always occurs when the supposed father is seeking custody or visitation, and the mother does not want him involved in her life. She will then dispute paternity, so as to challenge his claim to a right to custody or visitation.

Relationship to Child Support

Similarly, it is not necessary to establish paternity before filing for child support unless paternity becomes an issue. If the man being sued for child support knows without question that he is the father, there is no need for him to dispute paternity. All that would do is delay the inevitable order for support, and run up expenses for scientific testing that he will have to pay.

However, if the man believes that he is not the father, or believes it is possible that he is not the father, paternity will usually become an issue. Although some men will not put up a fight because they cannot afford the test, most will not subject themselves to years of paying support for a child that is, or may not be, theirs.

> **PARENT TIP**
>
> The husband will have to put forth strong evidence that he is not likely to be the father before a court will even order a blood test. This type of legal proceeding is complicated and should be done with the help of a lawyer.

ESTABLISHING PATERNITY WITHOUT A COURT PROCEEDING

Paternity may be established simply by the relationship of the parents; however, this does not generally apply to unmarried parents. The law provides that if the mother is married at the time the child is conceived, her husband is presumed to be the father of the child. This means that, until proven otherwise, the law will recognize the husband as the father.

In some states, California, for example, the presumption is *irrebuttable*, which means that under no circumstances will the law allow a blood test

> **PARENT TIP**
>
> Particularly in states having an "irrebutable presumption," if you are married and know your wife is having an affair, any delay in obtaining a divorce could increase the risk that you will end up financially responsible for a child that is not yours.

or any other action that is intended to prove that someone other than the husband is the father of a child conceived during the marriage. Therefore, if you are having an affair with a married woman and she becomes pregnant, you may not be allowed to claim the child as yours even if you want to do so.

Voluntary Paternity

Most states will allow a father to sign an affidavit to establish paternity, which eliminates the need for filing a court action. This is a written statement, signed before a notary or other official, in which the father acknowledges paternity. The affidavit must also be signed by the mother. Both signatures must be notarized and the affidavit must be filed at the courthouse. Paternity affidavit forms are available from the court clerk's office.

States encourage people to establish paternity using affidavits because it simplifies problems with inheritance, removes some of the lingering stigma that might plague children born out of wedlock, and avoids expensive and time-consuming court proceedings.

Establishing paternity can sometimes go a long way toward creating a meaningful relationship with a child. For this reason alone, if a father and mother are on good terms, establishing paternity through an affidavit is a good idea. Even if the relationship deteriorates, the father's rights are established. However, men should be cautioned that if paternity is established, they will be obligated to pay child support.

> ## PARENT TIP
>
> The fact that a person's name is on a child's birth certificate is not conclusive proof of paternity. There is no requirement that the father sign the birth certificate, so it is possible for the mother to list anyone as the father. With proper evidence, a birth certificate can be corrected.

Once the paternity affidavit is filed (and signed by a judge if required by state law), you cannot come back later and change your mind. No matter what information might arise to show that someone else is the child's father, the person who acknowledged paternity in the affidavit will not be removed as the legal parent of the child. If the father's name does not already appear on the child's birth certificate, the birth certificate will be reissued to show the names of both parents.

Should You Sign a Paternity Affidavit?

My advice to both men and women is—if you have any doubts, have a scientific paternity test performed. Asking someone to take a paternity test can open a can of worms, but it will be easier to do so sooner rather than later.

SCIENTIFIC TESTS FOR PATERNITY

Either party in a paternity action can request a scientific paternity test. Few paternity actions fail to utilize this most effective tool. Until recently, blood samples had limited usefulness. They could prove with a reasonable degree of accuracy that a man was not the father of a given child. However, they were totally ineffective when it came to identifying or pinpointing whether a given man was the father of a child.

However, with recent advancements in the use of DNA (genetic sampling), paternity tests have become almost 100 percent accurate in establishing that a man either is or is not the father of a given child.

The court will not automatically order tests simply because a paternity action is filed. There must be enough information in the prepared documents for the court to order testing. In addition, the court may require that evidence be presented at a court hearing before it orders the test.

If the court orders the test, the mother, child, and alleged father will all be tested at a court-designated laboratory. Generally, testing involves using a cotton swab to take a saliva sample from the mouth. A man found to be the father of a child will generally be responsible for paying for the paternity test. If he did not initiate the lawsuit, and is determined not to be the father, the cost is paid by whoever filed the paternity action. Prices range from $200 to $600. Check your medical insurance to determine if it will cover the cost of the test.

> **PARENT TIP**
>
> Because of the accuracy of DNA technology, the results of the paternity test will be conclusive, unless there is incredibly strong evidence to the contrary.

Challenging Test Results

If you believe the test results are not correct, you may challenge the results in court. The following are a few examples of the kinds of arguments that might be successful in challenging the results of the paternity test.

- ◆ The results were tainted by the lab. (You would need to prove that the lab was responsible for erroneous results in the past and that they routinely do substandard work.)
- ◆ The results were tainted by fraud. (An example might be that the opposing party sent someone else to take the test on their behalf.)
- ◆ You are physically incapable of conceiving a child.
- ◆ Someone tampered with the results.

PATERNITY LAWSUITS

If paternity is not established automatically, and if either parent is unwilling to sign and file a paternity affidavit, the only recourse is a paternity lawsuit. This generally involves going to court and asking a judge to determine whether the man is the child's father. This most often involves the judge issuing an order that a paternity test be performed.

Who Can Initiate a Paternity Suit?

The law only allows certain people to initiate a paternity suit. Such persons are said to have *standing*. This is a legal requirement that there be a certain connection between the child and the person filing the paternity suit.

If you believe you need to establish paternity, you must first determine if you have standing. Typically, the following people have the required standing which will allow them to file a paternity case:

- ◆ the mother of the child;
- ◆ the mother of an expected child;
- ◆ a man alleging that he is the father of the child;
- ◆ a man alleging that he is the father of an expected child;
- ◆ the child or the child's personal representative;
- ◆ a personal representative of an expected child;

- ◆ the mother and father of a child (filing together);
- ◆ the mother and father of an expected child (filing together).
- ◆ the state social service agency, which will usually intercede in instances where the child is receiving state or federal assistance; and,
- ◆ the prosecutor's office (or district attorney, state attorney, or some other name depending on the state), which will usually intercede in instances where the child is in need of services and will generally serve as the child's attorney in the action.

If you do not fall into one of the designated categories, you cannot file a paternity case. You can go through the trouble of having the papers drawn up and taking them to the courthouse, but once the court is aware that you have no right to bring the action, the case will be thrown out. (You could be ordered to pay the other side's attorney's fees for bringing the action when you had no right to do so.)

If You Are Not Sure the Child is Yours

You cannot file a paternity action if there is only a remote possibility a child is yours. Paternity actions are generally filed by people who want to prove paternity, *not exclude paternity.*

If you have not been asked to pay child support or otherwise been interfered with, you cannot file a paternity action—even if it is simply to satisfy your curiosity—unless the mother agrees to the action. In that case, it will not be necessary to file a paternity action; you can simply use the services of a private laboratory to have a scientific paternity test performed. Such laboratories are listed in your telephone directory under "Genetic Screening."

Effect of the Alleged Father's Death

In most instances, establishing paternity must be done prior to the alleged father's death. There are many reasons for this, foremost of which is that a deceased father cannot defend himself or challenge the evidence against him. If a paternity determination is sought after the father's death, the father must have done something to acknowledge the child prior to his death. For example, the father put his name on the birth certificate; put information in legal documents; or took some type of formal action.

Should You File?

Even if you determine that you have standing to file a paternity action, that does not mean you should run to the courthouse with paternity papers in hand. There are several factors you should consider before you do anything:

- *the consequences to you.* If you are the non-custodial father, the consequences may be paying child support or the other expenses associated with the birth and raising of a child. If you are the mother, you should be sure the alleged father is someone you want in your life and in your child's life for years to come. Tying your child to a deadbeat or uncaring dad may not be the best action or in the best interest of your child.

- *the impact on the child.* Let's say that the child is in an intact family and believes someone else is their father—someone with whom they have bonded, who is acting responsibly as their parent, and who is committed to the relationship. The child's best interest should always be at the forefront of any consideration that involves children.

- *seeing the process through to the end.* If the person you have filed the action against resists the action, establishing paternity can be a long and possibly expensive process. If you begin a paternity action, be certain you are prepared to complete the process.

- *handling the outcome.* Let us say, for example, that, as the alleged father, you have a three-year-old who was born out of wedlock, and for those three years you have been caring for and loving this child. However, in the back of your mind you have always questioned whether the child actually belongs to you. If you file a paternity action and find out the child is not yours, then what? Your emotional commitment and the feelings you have for the child will not go away. How will the results affect your relationship?

- *realistic expectations.* A paternity action, regardless of the outcome, cannot automatically create relationships or act as a form of punishment. Consider this example: John had been estranged from his children. He had vehemently denied paternity for years and resisted any attempt to have it established by the court or otherwise.

As he grew older, he required triple-bypass surgery. John then decided it was time to get right with the people he had wronged. When he was ready to acknowledge his children, they

PARENT TIP

The special relationship that exists between parents and children is not something that can be ordered by a court or decided by a jury. This relationship is something that must be tended to with time and attention.

were not ready to acknowledge him. He thought filing a paternity action would change things. Unfortunately, it made matters worse.

◆ *attempting to punish a parent who has had no relationship with his child.* Consider this example: Diane decided to file a paternity action. Her son was in his teens and she never needed child support because she came from a wealthy family. She had thought her child's father was struggling, but she learned he had married and had other children. Diane decided that filing a paternity action would be a way to punish him for abandoning her. She thought the public humiliation and embarrassment would cost him and his family. But, this was a painful experience that backfired.

PREPARING AND FILING LEGAL FORMS

The Parties
A paternity action or lawsuit is a civil action (not a criminal action). The parties will consist of the person who filed the case and the person who is denying paternity. In most instances the parties involved in a paternity action will line up in one of the following ways:
   ◆ *Mother of the child v. alleged father of the child;*
   ◆ *Alleged father of the child v. mother of the child;* or,
   ◆ *Child v. alleged father of the child.*

One variation is where a state agency (usually either a social service agency or the prosecuting attorney) files against the alleged father to get reimbursement for AFDC (Aid to Families with Dependent Children) benefits paid on behalf of the child. In such a case, the government attorneys will prepare and file the forms.

Complaint for Paternity

The *Complaint for Paternity* should include the following basic information:

- the name of the state statute which covers paternity actions; (Look for "Paternity" in the index of your state statute.)
- a statement regarding the length of time you have resided in the state and the name of the county where you are a resident;
- a statement regarding the length of time the opposing party has resided in the state and the name of the county where they are a resident;
- the child's full name and date of birth;
- your relationship to the child or unborn child;
- the opposing party's relationship to the child or unborn child;
- a statement that the child was or was not born while the mother was married to someone else;
- a statement regarding the status of any custody or visitation actions which may be pending or are waiting to be decided;
- supporting facts stating why you believe that you are or the opposing party is the father of the child; and,
- a statement requesting a blood test to establish paternity.

Motions

Paternity actions can also be initiated by using a form called a *Motion*. It uses the same format as the petition or complaint. A motion is filed when the parties already have an open case waiting to be decided by the court. For example, if a man receives legal papers asking that he pay child support, he might file a motion asking that paternity be established before he agrees to pay. Or, if a woman receives legal papers from a man seeking visitation privileges with her child, she might file a motion asking that paternity be established before she agrees to the visitation.

Summons
See Chapter 4 for information about the *Summons*.

Supporting Documents
The most common supporting document in a case to establish paternity is a certified copy of the child's birth certificate. You may also need a financial statement.

NOTIFYING NECESSARY PARTIES
You will need to notify all necessary parties of the court hearing. Exactly who must be notified may vary from state to state. The other parent will always need to be notified, and you may need to notify others such as the prosecuting attorney's office, state social services or AFDC office, and anyone else having legal custody or guardianship of the child. For more information, see the section on "Notifying Necessary Parties" in Chapter 4.

PREPARING FOR THE HEARING
The main evidence to be presented at the court hearing will be the results of the DNA or other scientific test for paternity. Therefore, you will need to obtain a copy of the test results, and possibly interview the person from the laboratory who will testify about the test. See Chapter 5 for more information about preparing for your hearing.

Presenting Your Case
The person from the laboratory who testifies about the test results will first need to be qualified as an expert. For more information, see the section on "Presenting Your Case" in Chapter 5.

The Judgement
For more information, see the section on "The Judge's Decision and Final Order" in Chapter 5. A sample completed *Paternity Order* is included in Appendix B. (see form M.)

–7–
CUSTODY

The word *custody* refers to the control or authority exercised by parents over their children. Generally, natural (i.e., biological) parents have equal legal claim to the custody of their children.

CUSTODY LAW AND PROCEDURE

Technically, without court intervention, a mother's claim to a child is not superior to the father's claim, nor is a father's claim superior to the mother's. In most jurisdictions, it does not matter that the parties were never married or that the father's name is not on the birth certificate.

Custody Terminology

Custody is a broad concept that refers to two things:

(1) physical custody or control over a child's person, in terms of where they live or primarily reside; and,

(2) custody as it relates to decision-making authority over things such as the child's education, religious training, and medical treatment.

When a child's parents do not live together, either because they have never been married to each other or because of a divorce, a court is often asked to decide the custody rights of each parent. The various state laws define and describe court-determined custody in different ways.

Traditionally, a court would grant one parent custody and the other parent would have visitation rights. In some states today, this is called *sole custody*. If one parent is awarded sole custody of a child, the other parent would not have to be consulted about major decisions affecting the welfare of the child.

To avoid such one-sided arrangements, many states have adopted the concept of *joint custody*. This may be called by various other names such as *shared custody* or *shared parental responsibility* (in Florida). In Texas, it is referred to a *joint managing conservatorship*. In some states, the decision-making aspect is called *legal* custody, and where the child resides is called *physical* custody. Wisconsin refers to decision-making as *legal custody* and to where the child lives as *physical placement*.

Some states allow joint custody only if it is agreed to by both parents. Other states mandate joint custody, unless there are extenuating circumstances that would make such an arrangement not in the best interest of the child. Courts try to divide the child's time between the parents in various ways such as six months with one parent and six months with the other parent; the school year with one parent and the summer months with the other parent; one week with one parent and one week with the other parent; etc.

You should not focus on the terminology used; instead, focus on what you want in the way of control over, and time with, your child. If you get what you want, it does not matter what the arrangement is called. For example, if you want your child living with you the majority of the time and you want input into decisions affecting the well being of your child, you should not spend a lot of time worrying about the legal terms.

Who Can File for Custody

Most state laws will only allow the following people to file for custody:
- the custodial parent;
- the non-custodial parent;
- the state or county child protective agency; or,
- anyone who has been caring for the child or who has exercised physical custody of the child.

Third-Party Custody

What happens if a father who has been out of the picture later discovers that the mother has lost custody of their child to a third party? The fact that one parent has lost custody of the children does not automatically mean the other parent has also lost custody. If the father was not named as a party to the lawsuit between the mother and the third party, and he was not officially served with notice, then the order does not interfere with his claim for custody of his children. Assuming he is fit, he has a good chance of being awarded custody. In order to obtain custody, he would need to file a motion asking the court to open the custody case between the mother and the third party or file a custody action against the third party.

Custody vs. Adoption

Some people get custody confused with adoption. The following are key differences between custody and adoption.

- ◆ Adoption involves and requires either the consent of the parents or the involuntary termination of parental rights. Custody decisions require neither.
- ◆ Adoptions are final. Custody decisions are never final and can always be modified any time there is a significant change of circumstances that affect the best interest of the children.
- ◆ Adoptions do not provide for the visitation of any parent losing parental rights. Custody actions provide for the visitation of the opposing parent.
- ◆ Adoptions require that a new birth certificate be issued reflecting the name of the adoptive parents. Custody does not affect birth certificates.
- ◆ Parents giving up or losing parental rights have no obligation to pay child support to adoptive parents. Custody frequently results in the non-custodial parent being ordered to pay child support.
- ◆ Adoption records are generally kept under seal. Custody records are part of the public record and are open for inspection by the general public.

◆ Generally, adoption proceedings are not adversarial hearings (although a termination of parental rights hearing may be). Generally, adoption proceedings are not adversarial hearings (although a termination of parental rights hearing may be).Custody involves court hearings and heated civil battles.

Resolving Custody Disputes

Unlike other forms of litigation, the primary focus in custody disputes is not on the two parties. In every state the guiding principle in custody determinations is what is known as "the best interests of the child."

In most custody disputes, neither parent is unfit to have custody. Instead, it is a matter of the judge weighing the various factors and deciding which parent will be slightly better able to meet the child's day-to-day needs. Just because one parent is awarded custody (or primary physical custody or whatever it is called in a particular state), it does not mean that the parent who was not awarded custody is unfit.

In situations where both parents are equally fit to care for their children, courts must consider other factors—many of which are beyond the control of the parties. They often include:

◆ *the child's preference.* Children who are of a sufficient age (which varies from state to state) are often given a chance to express their preference.

◆ *the status quo.* Most courts will not remove children from a place where they are thriving and developing normally. If a child has been with his mother for two years and the father decides he wants custody, he will have a heavy burden to overcome.

PARENT TIP

In attempting to provide judges with a definition of "the best interests of the child," many state legislatures have established a list of factors to be considered in making any custody determination.

- *parents are given preference over non-parents.* It is presumed that it is in children's best interest to be with their parents. However, that does not mean a parent has to be unfit to lose to a non-parent. The guiding principle continues to be whatever is in the child's best interest.
- *maternal preference.* This is still a viable notion in the minds of judges, although it may no longer be the law in many states. Judges prefer to keep children in their "tender years" with their mother.
- *gender.* Most judges also prefer to keep boys with their fathers and girls with their mothers, assuming that they feel that the same-sex parent can better provide the child with a role model of appropriate behavior.
- *primary caretaker.* The parent who provided for the child's day-to-day care will often have an advantage in custody determinations. Usually, this is the mother, but not always.
- *friendly parent preference.* Judges prefer to give custody to the parent who is the least hostile to the opposing parent. It is believed that it is in children's best interest to be raised by a parent who tries to get along with the opposing parent, as this will enable the children to have a relationship with both parents.
- *relationship with siblings.* Judges like to keep siblings together. They believe this provides a more stable living environment.
- *stability.* This is a major factor because judges believe children need to know where to call home. People who move around a lot are considered unstable. Instability is generally considered to be adverse to a child's best interest.
- *home studies.* Judges give a great deal of preference to the opinions of social workers. In many states, courts will order the parties to submit to a home study. The social workers visit the parties' homes and observe how the child interacts with each parent. They then submit a report to the court and testify to their findings.
- *smoking.* Recent reports that second-hand smoke can be dangerous to non-smokers has made smoking a consideration in custody

disputes. Although this has been considered in a few sensationalized cases, unless the child has health problems that would be affected, it is not likely that smoking will be a determining factor.

♦ *religious views.* The parties' religious practices only come into play when the views are proven to be adverse to a child's best interest. This is difficult to do.

Ten Commandments of Parenting

Judges look for basic parental qualities that are conducive to ensuring a child's best interest. The following factors are not engraved in stone nor handed down from on high, or even put into law. Still, I often refer to them as the "Ten Commandments of Parenting."

1. A parent shall spend quality time with their children.

2. A parent shall provide for their children's financial support.

3. A parent shall provide a stable living environment.

4. A parent shall provide for their children's spiritual well being.

5. A parent shall provide their children with moral guidance.

6. A parent shall create an environment in which their children can feel safe and free to express their feelings.

7. A parent shall provide wholesome and responsible discipline.

8. A parent shall thoughtfully consider and act in accordance with their children's best interest.

9. A parent shall be physically capable of providing for their children's needs.

10. A parent shall provide their children with unconditional love.

If Both Parents are Unfit

Filing for custody can sometimes backfire if the court determines that neither parent is fit to have custody of a child. The child may be removed from the home and placed in foster care or with relatives. Filing for custody is an invitation for the court to "pull back the drapes" and take a close look into the parents' private affairs.

Consider the following example. Brian filed for custody of his three young children. He made serious allegations regarding the fitness of their mother, his ex-girlfriend. The answer she filed was filled with equally serious allegations about his fitness as a parent. The court determined that both parents had drug problems and decided that neither parent was fit to retain custody of the children until they successfully completed a drug rehabilitation program. The children were temporarily placed with their grandmother until Brian and his ex-girlfriend received the treatment they needed.

Fatal Flaws

The factors listed above will be given varying degrees of importance depending on the other circumstances. However, there are several factors that are fatal to a parent's chances of gaining custody. The specific circumstances do not matter—if a parent is found to have one of these strikes against him or her, it will be very difficult to convince a judge to award him or her custody:

- drug abuse;
- neglect of a child;
- alcoholism;
- habitual criminal conduct;
- sexual abuse of a child;
- inappropriate sexual conduct; or,
- physical abuse of a child.

The Judge's Decision

Judges are given broad discretion in custody cases. Custody cases are rarely overturned on appeal. Appellate courts generally feel that trial judges are in the best position to determine what is in a child's best interest because they have an opportunity to see and speak with the relevant parties. No one knows this better than the judges. I was involved in a case where the judge made a determination I felt was erroneous. I asked him about it later in chambers. He said, "When I am in that courtroom I can do anything I want to do." He was right. Fortunately, most judges are more conscientious. States that allow attorneys to select the judge who will hear their case give parties an advantage because attorneys know which judges are more likely to rule in their client's favor.

The outcome of custody cases are hard to predict. I have one cardinal rule that I never break—never give a client a prediction regarding their chances of winning a custody battle. I adopted this rule early in my career and it served me well. After trying several cases I realized that we never know what's going to happen until it happens.

A court is not the ideal place to resolve a custody problem. How can a judge know what is best for a child he or she does not know and, sometimes, has never met? In most states, judges do not receive any specialized training in hearing custody cases. They rely on hunches as much as anything else. It might not be fair to say their decisions are often arbitrary, but that is so in many situations. It is amazing how honest and sincere people can appear when they are, in fact, telling a lie. Everyone can show up for court with a new dress or suit. Few alcoholics show up in court drunk and even fewer child molesters admit to having committed incest. Everyone seems nice, well mannered, and genuinely concerned about the child.

Death of the Custodial Parent

In cases where the custodial parent dies, the non-custodial parent's rights would take priority. Consider the following example. Marvin and Melanie had two children. They never married and the children were in Melanie's custody. Marvin had regular visitation through a court order, which he only occasionally exercised. When Melanie was diagnosed with a terminal form of cancer, she and the kids moved in with her sister. Her sister assumed the role of the children's primary caretaker. Melanie lived three years after moving in with her sister. Marvin continued to only occasionally visit with the children. He did, however, show up at Melanie's funeral and express his intention to assume custody of the children.

In most jurisdictions, as long as Marvin was deemed fit, he would be entitled to custody of the children. His rights would take priority over the children's aunt's although she had been caring for them. Marvin's sporadic visitation would not eradicate his claim to custody of the children. However, the fact that the aunt had been caring for the children would bolster her claim to visitation with the children.

What if Melanie had a will that indicated that she wanted her sister to be the children's custodian? Children are not property that can be passed through a will. If both parents die, courts will look to the will for direction as to who should care for children. However, the best interest of the children remains the guiding principle in custody cases, and it is presumed that if a parent is fit, children are better off with the parent.

Marriage or Divorce of a Parent

Unless there is something to the contrary in the judge's order, the marriage or divorce of either the custodial or non-custodial parent should have no impact on the rights of parents to custody or visitation.

Consider the following example. Ben and Abigail were never married. They lived together for ten years and had three children. After their separation the three boys lived with Ben, and Abigail was awarded liberal visitation privileges. The joint custody arrangement was necessary because Ben worked the third shift and Abigail watched the kids in the evening. Ben remarried and wanted to limit Abigail's visitation. The judge refused to do so.

Step-parents and Custody

If the step-parent wants custody or visitation after a divorce, separation, or death, the biological parents' rights will take priority over step-parents' rights. Unless the state recognizes the rights of step-parents, they will not have a legal claim to custody of a step-child. Their visitation rights will depend on whether or not a bond exists between the step-parent and the step-children.

Grandparents and Custody

There are two ways that grandparents can enter the picture. One is if the grandparents are fighting for custody; the other is if the grandparents seek visitation rights. Many states now have laws that recognize the rights of grandparents.

In most states, grandparents have the right to file for custody or for visitation privileges. These statutes specify the circumstances under which a grandparent may obtain an order for custody or visitation. Many of these statutes only provide for grandparent visitation where the parents are divorced or where one of the parents has died. If there is not such a statute, or if the grandparents don't meet the criteria of the statute, parents need not be concerned with the rights of grandparents.

There are many reasons why state legislatures have moved to recognize the place of grandparents in the lives of children. With the social problems associated with drugs and teenage pregnancies, more and more often grandparents have been placed in the role of primary caretakers for their grandchildren. Because of the emotional attachments that develop, states recognize that it would be in the grandchildren's best interest to have visitation with their grandparents. Courts realize that by recognizing grandparents' legal rights to visitation, grandparents are encouraged to take care of their grandchildren when it is needed.

Consider this example. Zach and Zora had lived together for thirteen years, and have two small children. They were both involved in drugs and eventually were arrested and sentenced to three years in prison. While in prison, the children lived with Zach's parents. After three years in prison, Zach and Zora were released and returned to live with Zach's parents and the children for another year. They eventually split up and moved into separate residences. They both filed separate custody actions against Zach's parents. Zach was awarded custody, and Zora and Zach's parents were awarded visitation. Zora was outraged that her visitation was limited somewhat because of the visitation that Zach's parents were awarded.

However, in at least two states (Florida and Tennessee), the state supreme courts have declared grandparent visitation statutes unconstitutional as violating the parents' right to privacy. The basic premise is that parents have a constitutional right to raise their children as they see fit, without interference by the government (as long as there is no abuse or neglect).

Although it is the grandparent seeking visitation, the use of a statute and the court system is the government interference. Even if you do not live in Florida or Tennessee, this argument may be raised if you find yourself fighting an attempt by your child's grandparents to obtain visitation rights.

> ## PARENT TIP
>
> Generally, grandparents are not awarded as much visitation as a non-custodial parent. Standard visitation schemes might include one weekend per month. In a visitation order, grandparents are not usually given any decision-making authority.

Children's Rights and Custody

Children's rights is an area that is growing in consideration. Consider the following scenario which is an example of how parents' rights and children's rights might collide.

Beth and Brian had been married for twenty years. They had three minor children. They divorced when their children were nine, eleven and fourteen. They went through a heated custody and visitation battle. Beth and Brian were awarded joint custody. The children lived primarily with their mother in a large metropolitan area and they were supposed to visit their father on alternating weekends and in the summer months. But they did not want to visit his home in a small rural area. In an interview during the case, the judge asked the children what they wanted. They expressed their dislike at the thought of visiting with their father, and the judge took their feelings under consideration, but he ordered the visitation.

The children visited for a few months, but the two older children then refused to go. Brian took the matter back into court and the court threatened to hold the children in contempt if they refused to visit. The children again resisted and the children were sent to a juvenile detention facility until they would agree to visit.

In instances where parents relocate, the court is required to reconsider the custody and visitation scheme to ensure that it is practical under the circumstances. Alternating weekends do not work in situations where the parents live on opposite coasts.

PARENT TIP

Once the child reaches the age of ten, courts will take what they want into consideration in terms of custody *and* visitation decisions. However, until they reach the age of majority, they will not be allowed to make decisions regarding their well being.

Most judges will order that neither parent can relocate without first obtaining permission of the opposing parent or the court. This is to protect the right of both parents to have contact with the children.

Courts usually condone relocating for educational or employment reasons. However, the court probably will not condone relocating to follow a boyfriend or to follow up on Elvis sightings. A parent who routinely relocates could be deemed unstable, and this could serve as the basis for the opposing parent to ask the court for full custody of the child.

EVALUATING YOUR SITUATION

Before filing for custody, there are several things you should consider to determine if filing is the best move for you, and if so, what is the best way to proceed.

Can you Reach an Agreement?

First, you may want to talk to the other parent to determine whether this is a matter that can be resolved without adversarial court action. If it is, then work together to draw up an agreement that is acceptable to both of you. The papers will still need to be signed by a judge and filed at the courthouse.

Consider this example. Don and Diane had been dating for twelve years and they had three children. Soon after their relationship ended, Don filed for custody of the children. He assumed that since he terminated the relationship unilaterally, Diane would not be open to resolving the custody of the children. Diane assumed that since she received the papers from the court, Don must not have wanted to resolve anything. Rather than talking to him, she contacted a lawyer.

On the morning the case was to be heard, Don and Diane ran into one another in the parking lot. Don said he was sorry that it had come to a court battle and Diane said she wished they could settle things. After talking a few more minutes, they reached an agreement. When they told the judge that their case had been resolved, he asked Diane why they had not worked it out prior to the court hearing. She said, "because he didn't ask."

Is a Dispute Obvious?

You shouldn't always let the opposing party know of your plans to file for custody. There are times when the element of surprise might work to your benefit. The following are a list of situations in which you should let the sheriff notify the other party for you:

- ◆ your child is being abused or neglected;
- ◆ the other parent has made it clear that he or she will never be agreeable to resolving the custody issue;
- ◆ the other parent has threatened to leave town with the child; or,
- ◆ the other parent has problems with confronting you.

What is in your Child's Best Interest?

Step back from the situation and make certain that doing what is best for your child is your primary motivation. It may be helpful to seek the guidance of people you respect and admire. If your child is old enough and mature enough to understand what is at issue, ask for his or her input. Do not put the child in a position of having to choose between parents, but ask them when they are happiest. Look at how they are doing in the current circumstances, and how filing for custody might affect their life or disrupt their routine.

For example, if you know your child has a learning problem that requires three or four hours of parent-assisted homework each night, and you work the second shift, it might not be a good idea to pursue custody. Or, if you have other commitments that make it impossible to give your child your full attention, perhaps you should not file.

If you are having continuing problems with the other parent, you need to be sure your reasons for wanting custody of your children are not somehow tied to those problems and your anger toward the other parent. You should not do something that will have such a significant impact on your children, since they have nothing to do with your adult battles.

What Does your Child Want?
While your child does not always know what is in his or her best interest, you should at least consider your child's wishes. The older the child, the more his or her desires should be considered. Seeking custody of a sixteen-year-old is probably not a good idea if the child does not want to be in your custody. At that age, they will usually do what they want to do and live where they want to live.

Are you Likely to Succeed?
There are custody battles that are so lopsided it is hard to imagine how they even made it before a judge. Do not file for custody unless you have a reasonable chance of success. Look again at the list of factors courts in your state consider when making custody awards (see the listing for your state in Appendix A). If you do not have any of those factors in your favor, maybe you should think a little longer and harder before making a decision about pursuing custody.

Are you Prepared for a Custody Battle?
Decide if you are prepared to follow the process to its conclusion. Custody cases tend to be very emotional confrontations. Custody actions also can be both financially and physically draining. If you

are handling the matter on your own, you still need to consider the time you need away from work for filing papers and making court appearances.

Are you Prepared for the Result?

You will need to prepare for defeat, as well as victory. Losing a custody battle can be devastating. But even if you are wounded, you still have a child that needs both parents. It would be a mistake to bow out of the picture because you have lost custody. Your child deserves more. You will still need to have a civil relationship with the other parent and to function as a mature adult with the responsibility of raising a child. If you win, you need to be prepared for taking on the obligations of a custodial parent.

When you file for custody can be important to your success, especially if your child is now living with the other parent. In most states, one of the factors considered by the courts in deciding the issue of custody is the length of time the child has been in a stable environment. Therefore, the longer you allow your child to remain with the other parent, the more this time factor weighs in favor of the other parent.

Consider this example. Bill and Betty have two children. They were never married and when their relationship ended, Betty was awarded custody. Betty got married, and there was evidence that her husband was an alcoholic and physically abusive to both Betty and the children. The children complained to Bill during their visits with him. Bill confronted the step-father and threatened Betty for three years that if she did not do something he would sue for custody. Finally, Bill filed for custody, telling the judge that the children were living in an abusive environment and had done so for the last three years. The judge asked Bill why he waited three years to do anything about the situation if it was so bad. Bill could not give the judge a satisfactory response and Betty retained custody.

Emergency Custody Orders

If you become suspicious that the other parent is planning to remove the child from the state, or relocate the child to a place that would make it difficult or virtually impossible for you to exercise your parental rights or sustain a relationship with the child, you should consider filing for a change of custody. Another alternative would be to seek a court order prohibiting the other parent from moving.

You can obtain emergency temporary custody until the court has an opportunity to conduct a hearing on permanent custody, but only if:

- ◆ the child is in immediate danger of abuse or neglect; or,
- ◆ the child is in danger of having their whereabouts concealed.

> ## PARENT TIP
>
> You should file a custody action if the child is in immediate danger of being abused, is being neglected, or if there is real danger of the other parent taking the child and going into hiding or leaving the country. In such cases, any delay reduces the likelihood of success.

Types of Custody Cases

Although there are numerous reasons for seeking custody, cases usually involve one of the following three situations.

1. There is currently no custody order, and one parent is seeking an

2. There is already a custody order, and one parent is seeking to change that order. This can be for several reasons, such as where the non-custodial parent wants to obtain custody, or where the custodial parent wants to obtain the court's permission to move out-of-state with the child.

3. There is already a custody order that one parent has violated. This is almost always where the non-custodial parent has refused to return the child to the custodial parent.

Obtaining Custody

In order to obtain a custody order, you must be the child's parent. If you are the mother, it would be extremely rare for your status as the mother to become an issue. If there is an issue as to whether you are the father, you will need to resolve that question before you may obtain a custody order. This can be done either by filing an affidavit of paternity (if the child's mother agrees you are the father), or by pursuing custody in connection with a suit to establish paternity.

Changing Custody

Custody decisions are never permanent, although it can be difficult to convince a judge to change custody. A custody order can be changed if there is a significant change of circumstances in the custodial home that adversely affects the best interest of the child. Ordinarily, the change has to involve the child, not just the living situation of the non-custodial parents. For example, custody will not be changed simply because the non-custodial parent has improved his or her financial situation so that he or she is now better able to provide for the child than the custodial parent. (Such a change in circumstances is more likely to result in an increase in child support for the non-custodial parent.)

Enforcing Custody

If there is already an order giving you custody, and the other parent refuses to recognize your rights as the custodial parent by such actions as refusing to return your child on time after visitation, or refusing to return your child at all, you may need to go to court to enforce your custody rights.

Defending a Custody Case

Do not panic if you receive custody papers from the sheriff or in the mail. The fact that a custody action has been filed against you is not an indication that you are unfit or that you will lose custody. Losing custody does not extinguish your parental rights or terminate your legal relationship to the child. It only affects your legal claim to physical possession of the child.

PREPARING AND FILING LEGAL FORMS

In the vast majority of custody actions the two opposing parties in the case will be one parent versus another parent. The plaintiff or the parent who files the custody action will either already have custody and want to keep it or they will not have custody and want it.

However, there are instances when the legal action will be between a parent and whoever has been caring for the child such as an aunt, uncle, or grandparents; for example, when one parent is deceased or otherwise not involved in the child's life.

The *Complaint for Custody* should include the following information.

- The state statute which covers custody actions. (Look for "Child Custody" in the index of your state statute.)
- A statement regarding the length of time you have resided in the state and the name of the county where you are a resident.
- A statement of the length of time the other party has resided in the state and the name of the county where they are a resident.
- Your relationship to the child.
- The name and date of birth of the child.
- Your relationship to the opposing party and or their relationship to the minor child.
- If the opposing party is not a parent, state the location or status of the other parent (i.e., the biological mother is deceased).
- Supporting facts stating why you believe it would be in the child's best interest to be in your custody. Try to do this without belittling the opposing party. If you cannot, state whatever facts you feel are needed to support your case. However, keep in mind that you will be given an opportunity to elaborate and go into specific detail when you get to court.

Summons

You will need to prepare and file a *Summons* along with your *Complaint*. See Chapter 4 for information about the *Summons*.

Supporting Documents

In addition to the *Summons* and *Complaint*, you will probably need to file some other documents. Which documents will vary from state to state, and possibly from one county to the next within a state, and even from judge to judge within a county. The forms listed below are the most common types you will find. Also, see Chapter 4 for more general information on legal forms.

UCCJA. The most common supporting document is the *Uniform Child Custody Jurisdiction (UCCJA) Affidavit.* The UCCJA has been adopted by all fifty states. Prior to its adoption, each state developed its own laws regarding custody cases. This meant if a parent did not like the custody determination they received in one state, they would simply take the kids and move to another state where they might receive a more favorable decision.

The purpose of the UCCJA is to reduce the likelihood of this occurring by requiring that courts cannot enter or modify a custody order until the child has resided in the state for at least six months and the court is made aware of any prior or pending custody disputes and of the names of any person who is not a party to the action but has a legal claim to the child. The UCCJA requires that an affidavit containing this information be attached to all custody or visitation complaints. Form G in Appendix B is a sample *Uniform Child Custody Jurisdiction Affidavit.*

Cover Sheet. See Chapter 4 for more information about cover sheets.

Financial Affidavit. While a *Financial Affidavit* usually relates to questions about child support, it may be required in a custody case for two reasons:

(1) to show you have the ability to care for the child you want in your custody; and,

(2) to be used when calculating child support for the other parent to pay in connection with you being awarded custody.

Filing with the Court Clerk

After you have prepared all of the documents that are required to begin your case, you will need to file them with the court clerk. See Chapter 4 for more information about filing with the court clerk.

NOTIFYING NECESSARY PARTIES

If you are the child's mother, you will need to notify the child's father that you have filed a case seeking custody. If you are the child's father, you will need to notify the mother. If the child is currently in the custody of any third party (such as grandparents, an aunt, foster parents, a child welfare agency, etc.) you will also need to notify that custodian. For more details about notification, read the section on "Notifying Necessary Parties" in Chapter 4.

PREPARING FOR THE HEARING

See Chapter 5 for more information about preparing for your hearing. In a custody hearing, you will be focusing on the factors used in your state to determine custody. These will include such things as your ability to care for the child and the other parent's lack of suitability to care for the child.

Presenting Your Case

For more information about how to present your case, see the section on "Presenting Your Case" in Chapter 5.

The Judgement

For more information about preparing the judgment, see the section on "The Judge's Decision and Final Order" in Chapter 5.

−8−
VISITATION

Of all of the types of legal procedures outlined in this book, visitation is usually the most simple. There are no mathematical formulas or charts to deal with, no complex set of factors for the judge to consider, no scientific testing, and no complicated testimony to be presented. It is usually a matter of you telling the judge what you want, the other parent telling the judge what he or she wants, and the judge deciding on a schedule that gives you an appropriate amount of time to spend with your child. Of course, as with any aspect of the law, it can get more complicated.

VISITATION LAW AND PROCEDURE
The law begins with the premise that the best situation for a child is to have frequent contact with both parents. The exception is where the child would be harmed, either physically or psychologically, by contact with a parent (this will be discussed later in this chapter). Therefore, absent any allegations of potential harm, you should be able to secure contact with your child, either in the form of custody or visitation. Since custody is covered in Chapter 7, this chapter will only deal with visitation. In all likelihood, you are seeking visitation either because you have been denied custody or you prefer the lesser responsibility of visitation.

Agreed Upon Visitation
If you and the other parent can work out satisfactory arrangements for you to spend time with your child, there is no need for a court proceeding. Such arrangements usually only work if both parents

recognize the need for the child to spend time with both parents, and can communicate with and be courteous toward each other.

For the parent with custody, being courteous includes agreeing in advance upon when visitation will take place, having the child ready at the time the other parent is to pick up the child, having the child properly clothed, being home at the time the child is to be returned, and being flexible to allow for the occasional late return or other circumstances that may develop.

For example, suppose your son was to be returned to you at 5:00 P.M. At 4:30 P.M. the other parent calls and tells you that his parents just arrived at his house and asks if he can return the child at 6:00 P.M. so your son can visit with his grandparents. This is a reasonable request that should be granted, unless you have another engagement planned or some other good reason it would be inconvenient.

For the *non-custodial parent*, being courteous includes agreeing in advance when visitation will take place, being on time to pick up the child, returning the child on time, returning the child with the clothing and other items he or she had when picked up, calling the other parent in the event you will be late or wish to change the return time, and being flexible to allow for other circumstances that may develop.

For example, suppose your son was to be returned to his mother at 5:00 P.M. At 4:30 P.M. the child's mother calls you, says that she is running late at a doctor's appointment. She asks if you can bring your son back at 5:30 P.M. This is a reasonable request that should be granted, unless you have another engagement planned or some other good reason it would be inconvenient.

Visitation works best under these circumstances. However, it seems that very few parents can make this work. In most situations, it is necessary to come up with a more rigid schedule. This can be done by the parents simply writing out a schedule and some basic rules, or it can be done more formally through a court order. Such schedules are discussed in the following section.

Visitation Orders

As stated earlier, it is a well-established principle in the law that it is in the best interest of a child to have visitation privileges with a non-custodial parent.

Visitation plans include the following:

- *weekends.* Visitation on weekends is the most common because children are not in school and most parents are not working. Generally, courts will order an alternating schedule that will allow both parents time to spend time with the child on their off days.
- *summer.* Summer visitation can vary in length from one week to the entire time the child is away from school. If the child will be with the non-custodial parent for the entire summer, the custodial parent might be awarded alternating weekend visitation. In essence, this reverses the custody/visitation arrangement for the summer.
- *child's birthday.* The non-custodial parent is usually awarded two to four hours of visitation on the child's birthday.
- *non-custodial parent's birthday.* The non-custodial parent is usually awarded two to four hours of visitation on their birthday.
- *Father's Day.* The child is usually allowed to spend Father's Day with the father.
- *Mother's Day.* The child is usually allowed to spend Mother's Day with the mother.
- *holidays.* It is typical for holidays to be alternated, so that the child is with one parent on one holiday, and with the other parent on the following holiday. The holidays may be reversed each year; for example, the child will be with one parent on Christmas Day one year, and with the other parent on Christmas Day of the following year. The following are other examples of how a court might address visitation over holidays:

- In even-numbered years, the entire Thanksgiving school vacation beginning at 5:00 p.m. on the Wednesday before Thanksgiving until 6:00 p.m. on the Sunday following Thanksgiving. The custodial parent will retain custody of the child for the entire Thanksgiving school vacation in odd-numbered years.

- The non-custodial parent visits with the child the first part of the Christmas school vacation each and every year beginning at 5:00 p.m. on the last day of school preceding the Christmas vacation until 1:00 p.m. on Christmas Day.

The visitation schedule should be fairly detailed so you and the custodial parent know what to expect. Generally, what is outlined in the order is the minimum amount of visitation you are entitled to receive. The custodial parent can always agree to give you more visitation than what is included in the judge's visitation order. However, you should adhere to the order as much as practicable.

Consider this example. Dean and Debra had two children together before their relationship ended. Dean was awarded custody of the children. The court gave Debra alternating weekend visitation. However, Dean routinely allowed Debra to visit whenever she wanted. The only time he limited her visits to the court ordered schedule was when he was angry at her for not paying child support on time or for not agreeing to babysit. Debra only insisted that Dean follow the order when she was mad at him and was certain that following the order would inconvenience him. The children were the ones hurt by their parents' conduct because they never knew what to expect in terms of when they were going to see their mother.

One benefit of following court-ordered visitation is that everyone will know what to expect. The custodial parent can make plans because he or she knows the children will be with the other parent. The non-custodial parent can make plans because he or she knows exactly when time will be spent with the children. Following the order will also reduce the chances of the non-custodial parent having to take the custodial parent back into court for failing to adhere to the visitation order.

A consistent deviation from the order can result in a modification, which might limit your visitation to what you actually do instead of what is in the court papers. For example, if the court order gives the non-custodial parent visitation every other weekend but they only visit one weekend a month, the custodial parent can ask the judge to change the order to one weekend each month. There is a good chance the custodial parent will succeed in having the visitation changed.

Progressive Visitation

There are instances when the court will make a progressive or gradual visitation schedule. Two examples include the following:

- ◆ the child is still very young and not old enough to spend large amounts of time away from the custodial parent; and,
- ◆ the relationship between the child and the parent filing for custody needs to be established.

An example of a progressive court-ordered visitation schedule follows:

For the first six months, visitation shall take place twice each week for four hours.

Following the six-month period and for the next two years, visitation shall take place on alternating Saturdays and Sundays for six hours on each day.

Thereafter, visitation shall take place on alternating weekends beginning Friday at 5 p.m. until Sunday at 6 p.m.

Overnight Visitation

Visitation schedules do not automatically include overnight visitation. Generally, most visitation plans do include some period of overnight visitation. However, there are instances when the court might not award overnight visitation.

◆ The judge believes the child is too young to stay away overnight from the custodial parent. Overnight visitation can be particularly troublesome in cases where the mother is breastfeeding.

◆ The judge believes the child needs time to bond with the parent before staying overnight.

◆ The parent who has requested overnight visitation does not have a suitable residence where the child may stay overnight. For example, a bed at the YMCA would not be considered an appropriate place for a young child to spend the night.

◆ The parent who is seeking visitation does not maintain a suitable environment in which the child should spend the night. For example, cohabitating without the benefit of marriage is still considered inappropriate conduct by many courts.

◆ The parent seeking visitation has not expressed an interest in overnight visitation.

If you want overnight visitation, come to court prepared to show the judge that you have a suitable home. Bring photographs of your residence and the room where the child will be sleeping. Whether you will need separate bedrooms will depend on the age and sex of the child. Courts will accept a teenage boy sharing a bedroom with his father, but are likely to reject a teenage girl sharing a bedroom with her father. Make certain you have purchased everything the child needs, such as a crib, high chair, or whatever is appropriate for their age. Be prepared to explain who lives in the home and who will be present during visits.

Supervised Visitation

Supervised visitation means that the visit must take place under the direct supervision of someone selected by the court. Such supervision is ordered by the court based on the judge's conclusion that the visiting parent poses some kind of threat to the child if not supervised. The issue of supervision usually arises when the custodial parent requests that visitation be supervised, or when a social worker recommends supervision. There are many reasons why someone might be ordered to have their visitation supervised.

◆ There is some question about the visiting parent's ability to care for the child. For example, the visitation by a father of a newborn may need to be supervised until the father becomes comfortable caring for an infant.

◆ There is a reasonable belief that the parent may abduct the child. Consider this example that involved a mother and father who had been in a heated custody battle. Before the judge could enter an order, the mother ran away with the child. Four years later she was caught and the father was awarded custody. The mother was granted visitation privileges; however, the court ordered that the visitation would have to be supervised to ensure that she would not again run away with the child.

◆ There is some indication that the child was sexually or physically abused. In instances where a child has been removed from a parent for abuse, supervised visitation may be necessary to protect the child.

Various people may be designated to supervise the visitation, such as:

◆ *the other parent.* Because this arrangement can create friction in an already hostile relationship, courts will usually only allow the opposing parent to supervise visitation if there is no one else available to do so. In cases where there are newborn children involved, the other parent may be the most practical option.

◆ *a social worker.* This person will be the likely candidate to supervise visits if a child welfare agency is involved in the case.

◆ *another third party.* Courts prefer people like grandparents, family friends, or someone else both parties can agree on to act in this role because the courts want to ensure that the visitation is a pleasant experience for everyone involved.

Visitation vs. Custody

Visitation is really a lesser form of custody. The time the child spends with you is your custody time. A parent who loses custody will usually be awarded visitation. The length of visitation and whether or not it will be supervised will depend on the circumstances of the case. The amount of visitation will be based on what the judge considers to be in your child's best interest. Typical visitation schedules include every other weekend and alternating holidays.

The biggest difference between custody and visitation is the length, or duration, of the custodial period. Generally, visitation is much shorter, although there are instances when the visitation can be quite liberal. In such cases the time a parent spends with their child might exceed the time a parent who has joint custody spends with their child.

Consider this example. Dave was granted visitation allowing him to visit with his children one evening each week, and every weekend beginning Friday and ending Sunday evening. He was also given one week during the Christmas holiday and eight weeks during the summer months. Don was awarded joint custody that placed his child with him for ten weeks during the summer months. Dave, who only has visitation privileges, actually gets to spend more time with his children than does Don who has custody. That is why you should not get hung up on the words.

Visitation and Child Support

You need to be aware of the fact that there is no direct relationship between visitation and child support. If the other parent is not allowing you visitation, you must still pay child support. Similarly, if the other parent is not paying child support, you must still allow visitation. The idea here is that the child's best interests are served by both visitation and support. Just because one of these is not being provided does not mean the other should be withheld. Your remedy in either case is to go back to court for enforcement of the court's order. The law in some states provides for child support credits for long periods of visitation.

EVALUATING YOUR SITUATION

Except where noted, this section is written on assumption that the child's father initiates the court proceeding. Situations where court action is begun by the mother or a grandparent are also discussed.

In General

There are typically three situations in which visitation is raised in court:

- ◆ there has never been a visitation order, and you are asking the court to make such an order;
- ◆ there is already a visitation order, and you are asking the court to change it; and,
- ◆ there is already a visitation order, but the custodial parent is not complying with it, and you are asking the court to order the custodial parent to comply.

Each of these situations may require a slightly different approach, and they are discussed below in more detail. Do not forget that you and the other parent can always agree to change the visitation arrangement.

In establishing an initial visitation order, or changing an existing order, you should first ask: *How much visitation do I need?* The general answer is: you need enough visitation to have a meaningful relationship with your child. Exactly how much time is required for this may be difficult to gauge. There are situations when children who live with both their parents spend little time with them because of the parents' career commitments. Especially as children get older, they may tend to spend more time with their friends than with their parents. People who have visitation sometimes spend more quality time than quantity with their children. At a minimum, parents should see their children at least once a week and every other weekend.

A related question is: *How much time do I want with my child?* The answer to this question will depend upon your situation, and may include consideration of such matters as the time you have available, your relationship with your child, and the intended activities.

Seeking Visitation

In order to obtain a visitation order, you must be the child's parent. If there is an issue as to whether you are the father of the child, you will need to resolve that question before you may obtain a visitation order. This can be done either by filing an affidavit of paternity (if the child's mother agrees you are the father), or by pursuing visitation in connection with a suit to establish paternity. Once the paternity issue is resolved, or if paternity is not an issue, you will need to give the judge a proposal for a visitation schedule.

Changing Visitation

The three most common reasons for changing a visitation order are:

- ◆ The child's circumstances have changed in such a way that the visitation order needs to be changed. This might include the child being older (appropriate visitation may be different for a six-year-old than for a fifteen-year-old), becoming involved in certain activities, or developing medical problems.
- ◆ The circumstances of one or both of the parents have changed (such as one moving further away) which require a change in the order.
- ◆ The order needs to be made more specific, to eliminate disagreements between the parents. The idea is to get an order that is very detailed and specific about all aspects of visitation, so that it is absolutely clear to both parents what is to take place. Of course, if the order is already quite specific, there is nothing that a new order can accomplish. In such a case, you will need to seek enforcement of the order, rather than seek a new order.

In the first two situations, it will be up to you to show that the circumstances have changed. This will usually be simply a matter of you telling the judge about the situation, and offering a proposal for a new visitation order that will solve the problem.

In the third situation, you will need to show that there are disagreements over visitation between you and the other parent. This will often be apparent from your case file, as there will be a record of previous court hearings in which you sought enforcement of the order. In such a case, it will be apparent to the judge that the existing order is not doing the job (or that more drastic action is needed to force the custodial parent to comply with the order).

Enforcing Visitation

Where the custodial parent is not allowing visitation according to the requirements of the visitation order, it is often necessary for the other parent to ask the judge to order the custodial parent to abide by the visitation order. This is typically done by filing what is called an order to show cause. Basically, the custodial parent is ordered to appear before the judge to "show cause" why she should not be held in contempt of court and placed in jail for failing to comply with the court's order.

As a practical matter, the custodial parent is rarely placed in jail. Jail only results when the custodial parent has prevented visitation repeatedly, without good reason. What usually happens is that the custodial parent explains why she denied visitation. This may be for a valid reason (see below on "Refusing Visitation") or for an invalid reason (e.g., the other parent has not paid child support or the other parent was late returning the child from the previous visitation period).

The judge will probably lecture the parents about the necessity to cooperate for the sake of the child, explain how he or she expects them to deal with the problem in the future, explain that he expects the order to be obeyed, and possibly modify the order to eliminate anything that may have been unclear or not sufficiently specific.

If you continue to have problems getting your visitation, it may take several such trips to court before the judge will take the drastic action of putting the custodial parent in jail until she agrees to comply with the visitation order. Almost all judges are more reluctant to put a woman in jail for violating a visitation order, than to put a man in jail for not paying child support. Another option for the judge would be to give you custody.

Refusing Visitation. There are two instances when a parent might be justified in denying the non-custodial parent their visitation.

- ◆ If the child is ill. A runny nose is not enough to justify refusing to allow the child to visit with the non-custodial parent. However, an extreme case of the flu would be enough to justify refusing visitation. If your child is ill, be courteous and notify the other parent before he or she drives all the way to your house to pick up the child.

♦ There is a legitimate concern that the child's well-being is in jeopardy. For example, if the non-custodial parent shows up intoxicated or without a car seat, a parent would be justified in not allowing the child to visit.

Use your best judgment. However, keep in mind that consistently violating a court order without justification could result in the child being removed from your custody, or you being held in contempt and jailed.

Defending a Visitation Case

If the other parent is seeks visitation which you do not want him or her to have, or if the other parent is accuses you of not complying with an existing visitation order, you will find yourself defending a visitation case. Your defense will be shaped by which of these situations apply. In both situations, your emphasis should be on what is best for your child.

In the situation where you are opposing the other parent's attempt to obtain visitation, you will need to explain (and present evidence) why the other parent should not have the visitation being sought. You may want to limit or restrict visitation from what the other parent is requesting, or you may want to totally deny all visitation. In either event, you will need to show that the visitation being sought would be detrimental to your child.

In the situation where you are being accused of not following an existing visitation order, you will either need to show that you did not violate the order or that you had a good reason for not following the order.

Considerations Before Filing

There are several things you should consider before filing for visitation.

♦ The amount of time you have available to spend with your children should be considered. If you work on the weekends, having the kids on the weekend does not make much sense, considering they will be with a babysitter most of the time. Moreover, if you work the third shift, it does not make sense to get the children for early morning visitation if you are going to be asleep for most of that time.

♦ If your work schedule changes, you may need to go back into court and ask that the visitation be changed to suit your schedule. Most courts will accommodate reasonable requests to accommodate your work schedule, but not your social schedule. The visitation may also need to be modified periodically to accommodate the other parent's schedule.

♦ Children's needs should be reasonably accommodated. If your child plays soccer and you cannot take them to the games, try to schedule visitation around the games. Some children's days are filled with more activities than their parents'; so be flexible, but do not allow your childrens' schedule to completely dictate when you visit with them.

♦ If you live far from your child, consider the cost and time associated with visitation. If you live across the country, it might not be a good idea to insist on alternating weekend visits. Be reasonable and remember there is no point in asking for or committing to more visitation than you can exercise.

PREPARING AND FILING LEGAL FORMS

You should file for visitation (or possibly custody) whenever the other parent consistently denies you regular and substantial access to your child. Few people are denied complete access to their children. In the majority of cases, however, non-custodial parents who have no court-ordered visitation are left at the mercy of the custodial parent. They are only allowed to visit when the custodial parent feels it is necessary and for as long as they feel it is convenient. As a result, the only time many non-custodial parents are assured of a visit with their child is when the custodial parent needs a babysitter.

You should also file for visitation if your paternity has recently been established, and you wish have a relationship with your child but the other parent has denied you visitation. If possible, you should try to have a visitation provision included in the paternity order, which will avoid having to go back to court, paying additional filing fees, etc.

The Parties

The parties in visitation actions are generally the same as those in custody actions. This includes the two parents, as well as any third party having legal custody or guardianship of the child.

The Visitation Complaint

The information that is included in the *Visitation Complaint* is similar to that which is included in the *Custody Complaint*. The *Visitation Complaint* should include the following information:

- ◆ The state statute which covers visitation actions. (Look for "Child Visitation" in the index of your state statute.)
- ◆ A statement regarding the length of time you have resided in the state and the name of the county where you are a resident.
- ◆ A statement as to the length of time the other party has resided in the state and the name of the county where they reside.
- ◆ Your relationship to the child.
- ◆ The name and date of birth of the child.
- ◆ Your relationship to the opposing party and or their relationship to the minor child.
- ◆ If the opposing party is not a parent, state the location or status of the other parent (e.g., "the minor child's biological mother is deceased.")
- ◆ Supporting facts stating why you believe that awarding you visitation privileges would be in the child's best interest. Again, try to do this without bad mouthing the opposing party.

Summons

You will need to prepare and file a *Summons* along with your *Visitation Complaint*. See Chapter 4 for information about the *Summons*.

Supporting Documents

Other than some type of cover sheet, there are generally no required supporting documents for any type of visitation proceeding.

Filing with the Court Clerk

After you have prepared all of the documents that are required to begin your case, you will need to file them with the court clerk. See Chapter 4 for more information about filing with the court clerk.

NOTIFYING NECESSARY PARTIES

If you are the child's mother, you will need to notify the child's father that you have filed a request to establish or change visitation. If you are the child's father, you will need to notify the mother. If the child is currently in the custody of any third party (such as grandparents, an aunt, foster parents, a government social services or child protective agency, etc.), you will need to notify whoever has custody.

THE HEARING

Scheduling a Hearing

For more information on how to schedule a court hearing, see the section on "Scheduling Court Hearings" in Chapter 5.

Notifying Necessary Parties

The parties you will need to notify are those who were notified when you filed your request to establish or change visitation. If you plan to have any witnesses testify, you will also need to notify them. For more information on notifying parties of court hearings, see the section on "Notifying Necessary Parties" in Chapter 4. For more information about notifying witnesses, see the section on "Witnesses" in Chapter 5.

Preparing for the Hearing

See Chapter 5 for more information about preparing for your hearing. In a visitation hearing, your focus will be on explaining what problems you have had regarding visitation and on proposing a visitation schedule. In most cases, you will not need any witnesses unless you expect the other parent to claim that there are no visitation problems. In such a situation, it may help if you can produce a witness who was there when you had problems with visitation.

Presenting Your Case

For more information about how to present your case, see the section on "Presenting Your Case" in Chapter 5.

The Judgement

After the judge announces his or her decision, you will need to prepare an order for the judge to sign. For more information, see the section on "The Judge's Decision and Final Order" in Chapter 5.

EXERCISING YOUR VISITATION

The key to visitation is exercising it. There are people who go to the trouble and expense of fighting to get visitation, then fail to follow through on it. Their job or other commitments get in the way. Failing to exercise the visitation you receive could result in one of the following:

♦ *your visitation privileges could be severely restricted.* For example, James was awarded liberal visitation privileges, which he exercised for the first six months after the visitation order was entered. Then he met a new girlfriend and his time with her began to encroach on the time he was supposed to be with his child. The child's mother filed a motion asking the court to reduce his visitation to the time he actually spent with the child. The court granted her motion.

◆ *the child will not want to visit* if he or she cannot depend on you to follow through on your commitment to visit. Your child might make other plans and may not want to follow through on the visits. It is best for everyone involved if the child looks forward to the visits. If the visits become disruptive, the other parent may move to have visitation restricted.

Forcing a Parent to Visit
A custodial parent can probably go to court to force the non-custodial parent to visit with the child. However, it may not be wise to impose your children on someone who has to be forced to spend time with them.

Forcing a Child to Visit
A common argument made by custodial parents accused of denying visitation is that the child does not want to go for visits with the other parent. Unless there is provable abuse involved, most judges will not accept this as justification for violating a visitation order. Judges will frequently tell the custodial parent that it is his or her duty as a parent to see that the visitation takes place. The parent is to be in control of the situation, not the child.

Responsibilites During Visitation
When the child is in your care you are free to do whatever you want with respect to caring for them. Unless the court makes an order to the contrary, you may associate with whom you choose, and you can leave the state temporarily (such as for vacation or to visit relatives). However, you must always act responsibly and maintain an environment that is conducive to the child's well-being.

–9–
CHILD SUPPORT

Providing financial support for a child is an obligation imposed on both parents by state law. Whoever has the legal status of parent, whether through biology or through the law, as with adoption, is responsible for supporting the child. It does not matter whether the parents are married, divorced, or were never married.

CHILD SUPPORT LAW AND PROCEDURE

This chapter concerns the situation where one parent is not helping the other to support their child. If you are not receiving financial help from the other parent, this chapter will explain how to go about seeking a court order requiring the other parent to contribute. If you have been served with court papers seeking to force you to pay child support, this chapter will explain what to expect and discuss how you might defend yourself.

If the parent with whom the child is living applies for welfare benefits (usually, Aid to Families with Dependent Children, or AFDC), the appropriate state agency will take action to try to obtain child support payments from the other parent.

If neither parent is able to support a child, they should seek government assistance, such as welfare benefits. If neither parent provides support for a child, the state child protection agency may step in to support the child and possibly charge the parents with neglect. Both of these situations are beyond the scope of this book.

A court may order a parent to pay child support to the other parent or to third parties. If the parent with whom the child is living is receiving AFDC benefits for the child, then child support payments will go to the government as partial reimbursement for the AFDC benefits. If the child is not living with either parent, then child support payments may be made to whomever has custody of the child.

Consider this example. Tim and Terri were never married and had three children together. Their relationship ended, and the children went to live with Terri. Three months later she was arrested and placed in jail. Tim's parents then filed for custody. Tim did not fight for custody because he assumed that as long as the children were not with their mother, he did not have to pay child support. Tim paid his parents on and off for a while but eventually stopped paying them altogether. Tim's parents took him to court and the judge ordered Tim to pay child support.

In many instances, regardless of who eventually receives the support, it is paid to a state agency which keeps track of the payments and disburses them to the proper party.

How Child Support is Determined
The two factors typically considered by courts in determining the amount of child support are:

(1) the financial needs of the child, and

(2) the financial ability of the parents to meet those needs.

Most states have created standard child support guidelines. These may be in the statutes or code, or may be created by court rule, a state agency, or some type of committee. They usually involve a chart or table, a mathematical formula, or a combination of these. Such guidelines attempt to calculate child support based on what both parents earn and how much they would spend on the child's needs if they were all living in the home together.

The guidelines are reviewed periodically to ensure that they keep pace with inflation and the cost-of-living in the state where they are imposed.

There are federal statutes designed to ensure that states work together in enforcing child support awards and to keep a person from avoiding their child support obligation by moving to another state.

Many states' guidelines use the following basic procedure to determine child support.

- Each party's *gross income* is determined. This is basically the income before any taxes or other items are deducted.
- Specified deductions are allowed, and subtracted from the gross income, to arrive at a *net income*. Deductions are typically allowed for such things as income taxes, social security, mandatory union dues, and health insurance premiums paid for the children.

> **PARENT TIP**
>
> State child support guidelines are designed to ensure fairly equal treatment of people throughout the state and to eliminate extreme variations that occurred when the amount was left up to the judge's discretion.

- The parties' net incomes are added together to arrive at a combined income.
- A table is consulted which uses the combined income to determine the financial needs of the number of children for whom support is to be paid.
- Each parent's percentage of the combined income is calculated, and applied to the needs of the children, to determine how much is to be contributed by each parent.
- Any of various adjustments are made to account for special circumstances.

There are several factors that child support guidelines typically take into account when calculating child support. These may include:

Income of the parties. The income of each party is usually the starting point, and the primary consideration, in determining child support. The following sources of income are usually included in determining gross income for child support purposes.

- salaries and wages;
- commissions and bonuses. One-time bonuses or income are included, but are usually distinguished from ordinary income.

For example, if you receive a one-time bonus of $50,000 in 1999, it will be included as part of your 1999 obligation, but it will not be used to determine the amount you pay in other years;

◆ overtime pay;
◆ dividends;
◆ severance pay;
◆ pensions;
◆ interest income;
◆ trust income;
◆ annuities;
◆ capital gains;
◆ social security;
◆ workers' compensation benefits;
◆ unemployment insurance benefits;
◆ disability pay and insurance benefits;
◆ gifts and prizes; and,
◆ alimony received. Alimony is usually only included as income if it is received from someone other than the opposing party or the party from whom you are seeking child support.

Health insurance. The amount being paid on health insurance for a minor child will be included in the child support calculation. The child support payment by the non-custodial parent will be higher if the custodial parent pays the insurance, and lower if the non-custodial parent pays the insurance.

Child care. Work-related child-care costs will be included in the equation. A person paying child support usually will not have to pay for any child-care costs in addition to the child support obligation.

Extraordinary expenses. If the child needs braces or special medical treatments for conditions such as asthma or psychiatric counseling, such considerations will be taken into account when calculating the amount of the child support. Other extraordinary expenses include those associated with special schools or travel expenses to visit each parent. The court will determine whether the expenses will be considered extraordinary.

Welfare benefits. Public assistance or Supplemental Security Income (SSI) are usually not considered as income, nor considered in any other way in child support calculations.

Automobiles and housing as compensation. Things provided by an employer, like automobiles or housing, will generally be included as income if they significantly reduce the living expenses of the person who receives them. For example, if you earn only $12,000 a year but your living expenses are only $300 a month because you do not have transportation, food, or housing expenses, then your income will be adjusted to reflect the items you receive as income.

Imputed income. Courts will base child support awards on imputed, or potential, income when it has been established that a party is purposefully suppressing their income in order to minimize their child support obligation. Imputed income is the income you could be receiving if you were to secure employment in a field that is compatible with your education, training, experience, or background. For example, if you are a doctor who quits his practice and begins working at a fast food restaurant three days after receiving notice that the other parent plans to seek child support, it is likely the court will calculate the child support amount based on your potential income as a doctor.

One instance in which a court will not use potential income is when a custodial parent takes a lower paying job or cuts back their hours to stay home with a small child (usually a child less than three years old).

Number of children. The number of children involved is considered in the equation. This may include the number of children of the person who will receive the support and the number of children of the person who is asked to pay child support. The calculations also take into account the number of children who are receiving child support through a separate court order. Money you are paying on your own, and not pursuant to a court order, will not generally be included as part of the calculation.

The following factors are generally not relevant in calculating child support:

- the age of the children;
- the age of the parties;
- the other financial obligations of the party paying or receiving child support;
- the relationship between the parties and the children;
- the financial strain placed on the paying party; and,
- the paying parent's need for the money.

> ## PARENT TIP
>
> Child support is based on the needs of the child and the theory that both parties should contribute something to the support of the children.

Consider this example. Max could not understand why he had to pay child support to his ex-girlfriend. They had two small children that lived with her. Two years after they ended their relationship she graduated from law school. She earned twice as much money as Max did. Three years after graduating from law school she married a doctor who made several times more money than Max did.

Max earned approximately $40,000 a year and was required to pay approximately $600.00 a month as child support. Max's argument was that since the children lived a more affluent lifestyle than he did, he should not be ordered to pay any child support. However, this is not the law. A person's child support obligation will not be extinguished by the fact that the opposing parent does not need the money.

Avoiding Child Support

If the custodial parent does not ask for child support or take you to court, generally, you do not have to pay. But, if you fail to pay, the custodial parent may come back at a later date and ask for more money. The child support may be retroactive and you may be ordered to pay for the years you failed to pay.

Basically, there is no way to get out of paying child support. Few people come right out and ask this question, but it is one that is in the back of the minds of many, and it manifests itself in the way

people behave—through purposefully suppressing income, conceal-
ing assets, or simply not paying. The repercussions for failing to pay
child support include the following:

* garnishment of wages
  and income tax refunds;
* revocation of profes-
  sional license; and,
* incarceration.

Manner of Payment

Child support payments
are generally made in
periodic payments on a
weekly, biweekly, semi-
monthly, monthly, or quar-
terly basis, depending on
your pay schedule. Generally,
buying clothes, food, and
other things children need in lieu of making actual child support
payments will not be acceptable forms of child support payment.

> ## PARENT TIP
>
> If the custodial parent informs you
> that child support is not necessary,
> you should get a written statement
> from the parent to this effect.
> Otherwise, the custodial parent may
> later go to court, asking that you be
> ordered to pay child support going
> back to the day the child was con-
> ceived.

Misuse of Payments

You may go back to court if you suspect that the money you are
paying in child support is not being used on behalf of the children.
In most states, the person receiving child support has no duty to
keep an accounting of how the money they receive as child support
will be allocated on behalf of the children. If you file, it is not likely
the judge will be able to do anything to change the situation. This is
not an unusual allegation, and more often than not, it is without merit.

The judge may lecture the opposing parent about using the
money for the child. If the children are being neglected and going
without food or clothing, the non-custodial parent may need to contact the state or county child welfare agency. However, this should
be done as a last resort and only when warranted, not as a form of
retaliation or punishment.

Additional Financial Assistance

One parent complained that although he made regular child support payments, the custodial parent regularly asked him for more money for things like piano lessons or school lunch money. Generally, a parent's child support obligation is limited to whatever is included in the child support order. They do not legally have to pay any more than the judge orders them to pay. However, parents should allow their conscience to be their guide. But keep in mind that any such financial assistance will be considered a gift, and you will not be allowed to have it credited toward the child support obligation.

Termination of Child Support

You have to pay child support payments until the earlier of one of these events takes place:

◆ the child is emancipated;

◆ you are no longer capable of paying child support;

◆ the child dies;

◆ you die;

◆ your parental rights are terminated;

◆ the child reaches the age of majority and is no longer attending high school;

◆ the child graduates from high school; or,

◆ the child becomes self-supporting.

Keep in mind however, that your child support obligation will not automatically go away. If you are under an order to pay, before you stop paying you should file a motion to have your payments terminated. If you stop paying prior to that time, you may suffer serious consequences.

Modification of Child Support

The amount of child support you are ordered to pay is not engraved in stone. It can be modified by the court to reflect a significant change in circumstances. The following events may trigger a change in the amount of a child support award.

◆ A significant increase or decrease (usually fifteen percent) in your income.

- ◆ An increase in the child's expenses. For example, the child support amount might be increased if the child needs braces or rehabilitation due to a car accident.
- ◆ You or the opposing parent has another child who you have the responsibility to support.

High and Low Incomes

Are you stuck with whatever the guidelines determine is the appropriate child support award? There are instances where you can petition the court to deviate from the amount determined by the child support guidelines. Most judges will deviate from the guidelines in situations where the parents have incomes that combine for more than a certain amount specified in the law (such as $150,000 per year), or incomes where parties earn at or below the minimum-wage earning level.

Child Support and Visitation

There are many instances when a custodial parent will not allow the non-custodial parent to visit until child support is paid. There are also cases when a non-custodial parent will refuse to pay child support until they have their visits with the child. Both parents in these situations are wrong. Child support is not a payment to see a child. Visitation is not a reward for paying child support. One really has nothing to do with the other. If you are ordered to pay child support you are obligated to pay regardless of whether you ever are allowed to see the child. If you are ordered to allow your child to visit with the other parent, you must do so even if you never receive a dime of child support. If you violate a court order, you risk being held in contempt and possibly jailed.

Child Support and Your Will

Your obligation to support your children ends with your death. You do not have to provide for your children in your will. With respect to your children, you are free to divide your estate in any way you decide is appropriate.

EVALUATING YOUR SITUATION

There are basically three things you need to know in order to calculate child support:

1. your income;
2. the other parent's income; and,
3. your state's child support guidelines.

From your pay stubs for this year, and from last year's W-2 form and income tax return, you should know your gross income. If you are the custodial parent, you will also have a good idea of the cost of health insurance, day care, and other special needs of your child. Unless you happen to know what the other parent earns, you will just have to estimate what he or she earns. (Refer to the section of this chapter on "How Child Support Is Determined," as well as your state's support guidelines, for more information on what constitutes income, how net income is determined, etc.)

Once you determine the income for you and the other parent, you need to plug that information into your state's child support guidelines or formula to get an estimate of how much child support is likely to be ordered. Because each state's child support guidelines are different, it is impossible to be more specific here. (See the listing for your state in Appendix A for information about where to find your state's child support guidelines.)

· PARENT TIP

In most cases there will not be much room for argument about child support. The child support guidelines or formula will be applied to the incomes of you and the other parent, and the child support amount determined mathematically. The only places for argument will be whether you or the other parent accurately reported income, and whether there are any special needs of your child that require additional child support.

Seeking Child Support

If a child support order is being sought for the first time, the incomes of the parties and the child support guidelines will determine the amount of child support to be paid.

Changing Child Support

In order to increase or decrease child support, the person seeking the change will need to show that financial circumstances have changed since the current child support order was issued. In most cases, this will mean showing that there has been a significant change in the income of at least one of the parents. If you want an increase in child support, you will need to show that the other parent's income has increased, or that your income has decreased. If you want a decrease in child support, you will need to show that your income has decreased, or the other parent's income has increased. If the current order was above the regular child support schedule because your child had special needs, a change in those special needs could also be a basis for a change in child support.

Enforcing Child Support

All states have a state agency designated to enforce child support orders on behalf of custodial parents who receive AFDC benefits. Usually the collection services of that agency is also available to other custodial parents who request services.

Defending a Child Support Claim

If you are being sued for child support, there is little you can do to completely avoid child support. If you do not believe the child is yours, you can dispute paternity. This will usually lead to a paternity action being filed against you, which is discussed in detail in Chapter 6. The only other way you might avoid a child support order is if you are receiving some type of welfare benefits as your only source of income. See the section of this chapter on "How Child Support Is Determined" for more information on what type of benefits do and do not constitute income for child support purposes.

In most cases, what you will be arguing about is the *amount* of child support. There are only three things that can be argued here:

1. your income is actually less than stated by the other parent or in a report from an investigator;
2. the other parent's income is actually more than stated by the other parent or in a report from an investigator; or,
3. the child's special needs are less than stated by the other parent or in a report from an investigator.

In a case involving a request to raise or lower child support, in addition to the matters mentioned above, you can also argue either that there has been no change since the last order was issued, or that the change in income or needs is so small that it does not merit a change in the child support amount.

PREPARING AND FILING LEGAL FORMS

The parties in child support disputes will generally include the custodial parent or whoever has custody of the child, and the non-custodial parent.

Child Support Complaint

The following information should be included in the *Child Support Complaint:*

- ♦ the state statute which covers child support actions (look for "Child Support" in the index to your state statute);
- ♦ the length of time you have resided in the state and the name of the county where you are a resident;
- ♦ the length of time the other party has resided in the state and the name of the county where they are a resident;
- ♦ your relationship to the minor child;
- ♦ the child's name and their date of birth;
- ♦ a statement regarding the defendant's relationship to the minor child;
- ♦ a statement regarding when and how you obtained custody of the minor child;
- ♦ a statement that the defendant is able-bodied, employed and capable of providing child support;

- ◆ a statement that the child is in need of support; and,
- ◆ a statement regarding whether the child has any extraordinary expenses.

Summons
If you are seeking an initial child support order, you will need to prepare and file a *Summons* along with your *Child Support Complaint*. See Chapter 4 for information about the *Summons*.

Supporting Documents
In addition to some type of cover sheet, the most common supporting document in a child support case is the *financial affidavit*. Many states have their own form, so be sure to check with the court clerk. This type of form has different names in different states, such as *Financial Statement*, *Financial Affidavit*, or *Statement of Net Worth*.

Filing with the Court Clerk
After you have prepared all of the documents that are required to begin your case, you will need to file them with the court clerk. See Chapter 4 for more information about filing with the court clerk.

NOTIFYING NECESSARY PARTIES
Whether you are seeking to establish child support, or seeking to increase or decrease child support, you will need to notify the other parent. If you are seeking a decrease and the other parent is receiving AFDC benefits for the child, you may also need to notify the state social service agency managing the AFDC program.

THE HEARING

Scheduling a Hearing
For more information on how to schedule a court hearing, see the section on "Scheduling Court Hearings" in Chapter 5.

Notifying Necessary Parties

The parties you will need to notify are those who were notified when you filed your request to establish or change child support, as well as any witnesses you intend to have testify. In child support cases, the most common witnesses are employers, or other third parties who can verify the income of the other parent. For more information on notifying parties of court hearings, see the section on "Notifying Necessary Parties" in Chapter 4. For more information about notifying witnesses, see the section on "Witnesses" in Chapter 5.

Preparing for the Hearing

See Chapter 5 for more information about preparing for your hearing. In a child support case, the primary emphasis will be on the accuracy of the income information of you and the other party. In some cases, you may also need to establish the special needs of a child.

Presenting Your Case

For more information, see the section on "Presenting Your Case" in Chapter 5.

The Judgement

After the judge announces his or her decision, you will need to prepare an order for the judge to sign. For more information, see the section on "The Judge's Decision and Final Order" in Chapter 5.

–10–
TERMINATION OF PARENTAL RIGHTS

Termination of parental rights is a court action that severs all legal ties between the parent and the child, and is considered to be one of the most severe court actions that can be brought against a parent. Once parental rights are terminated, there is no way to revive the legal ties between a parent and child (except through an adoption; however, it is highly unlikely that a court would approve an adoption by a parent whose parental rights were terminated).

TERMINATION OF PARENTAL RIGHTS LAW AND PROCEDURE

Although the results are severe, proceedings for termination of parental rights are fairly common in the following situations:

- ◆ in adoption proceedings when the biological parent will not consent to the adoption or a biological parent cannot be located; or,
- ◆ in cases of severe abuse or neglect, when the child protection agency believes the chances of reuniting the child and the parents are so hopeless that the child should be placed for adoption.

Termination of parental rights actions gained a lot of notoriety in the case of Gregory K. He was the young man who hired a lawyer to terminate his parents' rights so his foster family could adopt him. The state law would not allow the foster parents to bring an action, so Gregory K had to bring an action on his own behalf.

Another highly publicized termination of parental rights case was the one in which two babies were switched at birth. When one of the children became ill and died, the parents discovered the child did not belong to them. They went in search of their child, and when they found her, she did not want to be reunited with them. The child filed papers to have her biological parents' rights terminated so that she could remain with the family that had raised her.

Termination of parental rights is a civil proceeding. Generally, the proceeding is held in closed session which means, unlike most cases, the general public will not be allowed to sit in on the hearings. A closed session is considered necessary in termination of parental rights cases because the facts are sensitive and it is necessary to protect the privacy and identity of the children.

Because the consequences of a termination proceeding are severe, the court can appoint an attorney to represent the person whose rights are subject to being terminated in the proceeding. The person initiating the termination proceeding must prove the case with clear and convincing evidence. This standard of proof is higher than the traditional standard in civil cases (called on a preponderance of the evidence) because the state legislature wants to make it difficult to terminate parents' rights. Generally, the termination proceeding will be presided over by a judge, not a jury.

You can appeal the judge's decision. However, unless the judge clearly abuses his discretion, it is not likely that the appeal will be successful.

Who Can Seek Termination of Parental Rights

The following people and organizations can terminate the parental rights action.

- *the state or county child welfare agency*. These agencies are responsible for initiating the majority of termination of parental rights proceedings—it is their responsibility to protect children. The child welfare agency is likely to have the information and evidence that will support a finding that a parent's rights should be terminated. The agency moves to terminate parental rights in cases when it is believed that such action will protect the child.

- *a custodial parent*. The parent who has been caring for the child can move to have the other parent's rights terminated.

◆ *a guardian ad litem.* This is someone who has been appointed by the court to represent the child's best interest and to act on their behalf. In most jurisdictions, children are not prohibited from initiating termination of parental rights actions. However, children usually do so through the appointment of a guardian ad litem or by having some adult acting on their behalf.

> # PARENT TIP
>
> Child welfare agencies will usually work to help parents learn to properly care for their child before they will move for a termination of parental rights. It is the state's interest to restore families and keep children with their parents.

◆ *a person seeking to adopt the child.*

◆ *grandparents or other members of the child's extended family.*

◆ *a person with knowledge of the fact alleged in the complaint seeking to terminate the parent's rights.*

◆ *any "interested person" or a person with a "legitimate interest" in the child's well being.*

Most states do not allow foster parents to move to terminate the rights of the children's parents. Children are placed in foster care while their parents get their act together. It is believed parents will resist getting help if they believe they could lose custody to a foster parent.

Effect on the Other Parent

Terminating the rights of one parent has no impact on the other parent's rights, unless both parents were parties in the termination proceeding. The facts might exist to justify terminating the rights of one parent but not the rights of the other.

Grounds for Terminating Parental Rights

Each state legislature designates a set of grounds that will support a finding to terminate a parent's rights. Generally, the law will only require that one of the grounds be established or proven. However, it is always a good idea to establish as many of the grounds on the list as possible. Sometimes the cumulative effect of the evidence can go a long way in establishing that a parent's rights should be terminated. The following are some of the more common grounds for termination of parental rights:

Abandonment. The general rule is that a parent who abandons their child for six months or longer is subject to having their parental rights terminated.

Abandonment can come in two forms. The first is called *physical abandonment.* An example might be a situation in which a couple breaks up, and the children are placed in the custody of the mother. The father is awarded visitation, and after a few months the father stops visiting and simply drops out of the picture. He does not call, make visitation arrangements, or send any child support payments.

The other form of abandonment is referred to as *constructive abandonment.* One court explained it as what takes place "is a parent withholds his presence, his love, his care, the opportunity to display filial affection and willfully neglects to lend support and maintenance." Even if you are physically present but do not perform the function of a parent, you could be held to have constructively abandoned your child.

Constructive abandonment is a form of neglect. For this reason a parent who has a child in foster care and fails to follow through on the steps needed to have the child returned to them might be considered to have abandoned the child.

PARENT TIP

State law requires that certain "grounds" or circumstances exist before a person can seek to have a parent's rights terminated. A child that is not happy with the rules his parents impose can not move to have his parents rights' terminated. Nor would a parent who does not wish to pay child support be able to have his or her parental rights terminated.

One of the key components of both forms of abandonment is that the conduct of the parent must be *willful*. There must be some proof that the reason the parent is not physically or emotionally present for their children is because they choose not to be. For example, it is not abandonment if a parent is not aware of where their children live because the opposing parent has concealed their whereabouts, or if limited resources keep them from supporting or visiting. If a parent is doing the best they can under the circumstances, it is not likely they will be found to have abandoned a child.

Failing to Acknowledge Paternity*.* Failing to acknowledge paternity within six months after the child's birth might be grounds for terminating their parental rights. However, before a man's rights can be terminated on this basis, it must be shown that he knew or had reason to know that he was the father of the child.

Incarceration*.* In some states, a parent's incarceration is grounds for the termination of parental rights. However, in most jurisdictions just being incarcerated is not enough. The courts consider three factors in determining whether the parent's incarceration should be enough to support the termination of parental rights.

- ◆ What was the situation before the parent was incarcerated? If the parent did not pay child support or only did so sporadically, and visited sporadically prior to the incarceration, it is more likely the incarceration will be deemed abandonment and a judge will be inclined to terminate the parental rights. However, if the parent was a consistent and positive presence in the child's life prior to going to jail, it is not likely the court will terminate that parent's rights on the basis of incarceration.

- ◆ How willing is the parent to rehabilitate and behave in a way that reflects concern about the child's best interest? If there is a situation where a parent has an isolated incident of incarceration, gets out of jail, and behaves properly, it is not likely that the parental rights will be terminated on the basis of their incarceration. However, if the parent is a career criminal and repeat offender and does not show any inclination or interest in becoming a law-abiding citizen, the court is more likely to terminate the parental rights.

◆ How long is the sentence the parent received? The longer the sentence the parent receives the more likely the court will terminate the parental rights. If they receive a life sentence without the possibility of parole, it is difficult to imagine how they will be deemed not to have abandoned their child. However, a sentence of shorter duration might not be enough to support a finding of termination of parental rights.

Mental Incapacity. Mental incapacity can come in the form of mental illness or mental retardation, and must exist to the extent that it renders the parent unable to care for the child. Most states do not require the person to have been determined incompetent by a court of law or to have a condition that is universally recognized in the psychiatric community. In termination proceedings, courts focus on the parent's ability to care for the children. There is usually a requirement that the mental incapacity be a permanent condition or one that is not likely to be cured or corrected in the immediate future.

Establishing mental incapacity will ordinarily require the expert testimony of a psychiatrist or psychologist. The testimony of a social worker or the opposing parent alone will not be sufficient.

Neglect. Neglect allegations focus more on the condition of the children than any specific conduct of the parent. For example, a parents addiction to drugs is alone not enough to terminate parental rights. However, it is when the addiction negatively impacts the ability to care for the children that it becomes neglect and can result in the termination of parental rights.

Almost every petition to terminate parental rights will include neglect allegations. Neglect has been used to support a finding that parental rights should be terminated based on the following allegations.

◆ A parent failed to provide child support required by a court order. Parents are expected to use the financial resources at their disposal to support their children.

◆ A parent allowed her young children to stay at home alone for several hours at night while she went out with friends.

- A parent failed to provide children with food and appropriate clothing, routinely sending his child to school without a coat during the winter months and without lunch money.
- A parent failed to protect his children from abuse inflicted by the other parent.

Abuse. Physical and sexual abuse both are grounds for the termination of parental rights. In many jurisdictions an isolated instance of abuse, if sufficiently extreme, can support a finding that a parent's rights should be terminated.

Because of the severity of these allegations, courts usually will intervene more rapidly to protect the children from future danger, especially in the presence of testimony that the parent is not likely to benefit or has not benefited from counseling or has failed to take steps to minimize future abuse.

Defenses

The best way to defend against a termination of parental rights action is to show the court that terminating parental rights will have an adverse impact on the child. Provide evidence of a loving relationship between parent and child, despite whatever evidence there may be to the contrary. For example, a parent who has not paid child support could argue that they have visited regularly and are a positive influence on the child.

A parent whose rights are subject to termination might show that there has been a significant change since the complaint or petition was filed. For example, a parent could show evidence that they have undergone drug rehabilitation or corrected whatever problems that existed prior to and at the time the petition was filed. It would be a good idea to have testimony from experts to corroborate the change and testify to the unlikeliness of the behavior reoccurring.

The best defense to a termination of parental rights action may be a clean suit and a sob story. Courts are reluctant to terminate parental rights and are generally looking for reasons not to terminate. If you can convince the judge of your love and future commitment to caring for the child, you are likely to be able to convince them not to terminate.

The Court Decision

The judge who presides over a termination of parental rights proceeding must find two things:

1. the person who filed the petition has established the grounds cited in the statute (see Appendix A); and,
2. terminating parental rights will be in the child's best interest.

If both of these elements are not present, the judge has no authority to terminate the parent's rights. Courts are given discretion, but even if they feel terminating would be in a child's best interest they cannot terminate the parent's rights unless at least one of the grounds is proven. Nor can the judge terminate if the grounds exist to terminate, but termination is not in the child's best interest.

Courts are more likely to terminate the parental rights of a parent in situations when someone is waiting to adopt the child, whether it is a step-parent adoption or a private adoption. The court doesn't want to leave children without a parent or to condemn them to a life in the foster care system.

Once the final order terminating parental rights is entered, it ends the parent's obligation to pay child support and extinguishes their right to visit or have a relationship with the child. Their consent will no longer be needed for adoption. It also terminates the parent's right to inherit from the child. However, in most jurisdictions the child will continue to be entitled to inherit from the parent even after their parental rights are terminated until the child is adopted or reaches the age of majority.

PREPARING AND FILING LEGAL FORMS

The following are examples of why a parent might file a termination of parental rights action against the other parent.

- ◆ He or she does not want the parent who has abandoned the child for several years to show up and disrupt the child's life.
- ◆ He or she is ill and want to ensure that if something happens to him or her, the child will go to someone other than the other parent.
- ◆ He or she wants the child to be adopted by a step-parent.

◆ The child is wealthy and the filing parent doesn't want the parent who has abandoned the child to have access to the child's assets.

The Parties

The parties in a petition to terminate parental rights will usually line-up this way:

> *Custodial Parent v. Non-Custodial Parent*
>
> *Prospective Adoptive Parent v. Non-Custodial Parent*
>
> *Child Welfare Agency v. Parents*

Petition to Terminate Parental Rights

The following information should be included in the *Petition to Terminate Parental Rights:*

◆ the name of the state statute which governs termination of parental rights actions (look for "Termination of Parental Rights" in the appendix to your state statute);

◆ the name of the minor child who is the subject of the petition and his date of birth;

◆ the respondent's relationship to minor child;

◆ the state where the respondent resides and how long they are believed to have resided there;

◆ the petitioner's relationship to the minor child;

◆ the state where the petitioner resides and how long they are believed to reside there prior to the filing of the petition;

◆ the relationship between petitioner and respondent, if any;

◆ a statement regarding whether anyone has been appointed as guardian *ad litem* for the child in this or any other action;

◆ the reasons the respondent's rights are subject to being terminated (refer to Appendix A); and,

◆ a statement that the petition has not been filed to circumvent the provisions of the Uniform Child Custody Jurisdiction Act.

Summons

You will need to prepare and file a *summons* along with your *petition to terminate parental rights*. See Chapter 4 for information about the *summons*.

Supporting Documents

Other than some type of cover sheet, there are not usually any supporting documents filed with a *petition to terminate parental rights*.

Filing with the Court Clerk

After you have prepared all of the documents that are required to begin your case, you will need to file them with the court clerk. See Chapter 4 for more information about filing with the court clerk.

NOTIFYING NECESSARY PARTIES

In all cases you will need to notify the other parent. If the other parent cannot be located, you will probably need to publish a notice in a newspaper. Of all of the various types of legal proceedings involving parents, the termination of parental rights is probably the most serious. Therefore, it is absolutely essential to properly notify all of the necessary parties.

THE HEARING

Scheduling a Hearing

For more information on how to schedule a court hearing, see the section on "Scheduling Court Hearings" in Chapter 5.

Notifying Necessary Parties

The parties you will need to notify are those who were notified when you filed your petition to terminate parental rights, as well as any witnesses you intend to have testify. For more information about notifying parties, see the section on "Notifying Necessary Parties" in chapter 4. For more information about notifying witnesses, see the section on "Witnesses" in Chapter 5.

Preparing for the Hearing

See Chapter 5 for more information about preparing for your hearing. In a termination of parental rights case, the primary emphasis will be on proving one or more of the grounds listed in your state's laws which will justify termination.

Presenting Your Case

For more information about how to present your case, see the section on "Presenting Your Case" in Chapter 5.

The Judgement

After the judge announces his or her decision, you will need to prepare an order for the judge to sign. For more information, see the section on "The Judge's Decision and Final Order" in Chapter 5.

GLOSSARY

A

abandonment. The withholding of contact, love and/or financial support from a minor child. Abandonment is grounds for the termination of parental rights. Before a court will terminate a parents rights' on these grounds, there must be a showing that his/her conduct is willful or intentional. A parent cannot be found to have abandoned a child he did not know existed.

abuse. Any conduct by a parent that endangers the physical and emotional well being and development of his/her child. Abuse can take many forms including physical assault, verbal attacks or inappropriate sexual contact. A single instance of abuse, depending on its severity, can be grounds for terminating parental rights.

adoption. Court action that results in the creation of a parent/child relationship where it did not previously exist. A minor child cannot be adopted unless his parents give their consent, are deceased or their rights are terminated. An adoptive parent has the same rights and responsibilities as a biological parent.

AFDC (Aid to Families with Dependent Children). A form of welfare benefits. Generally, if a custodial parent is receiving AFDC the appropriate state agency will pursue the non-custodial parent to pay child support and possibly reimburse the government for the payments made on behalf of the minor child.

arrears. Unpaid child support payments. A parent who falls too far behind in child support payments is subject to having his/her paycheck and income tax return garnished and/or imprisonment.

automatic paternity. Paternity that is presumed as a consequence of the relationship of the parties. A man does not have to submit to a test to establish paternity of a child his wife conceived during their marriage.

B

best interest of the child. Often referred to as the "polar star", it is the compass judge's follow when making decisions regarding custody, visitation and termination of parental rights.

biological parents. The two people responsible for conceiving a child. Also referred to as *birth parents* or *natural parents*.

birth parents. See *biological parents*.

C

change of circumstances. In most jurisdictions a court must find that there has been a significant change of circumstances before it will modify an existing custody order. Generally, the change of circumstances must relate to a condition or situation in the custodial home which adversely impacts the best interest of the child.

child support. The amount of money a non-custodial parent is obligated to pay on behalf of his/her minor child(ren).

child support guidelines. A mathematical formula which is created by a state's legislature and used to determine a non-custodial parents child support obligation.

civil contempt. When a party fails to do what the court ordered him or her to do. Civil contempt is punishable by fine and/or imprisonment.

clear and convincing evidence. It is the standard of proof in termination of parental rights cases. Before an opposing party can succeed in terminating a parents' parental rights, he/she must establish by clear and convincing evidence that there are grounds to do so.

code. See *statutes*.

complainant. The party who initiates or originally files the court action.

complaint. The document the complainant or petitioner files to begin the legal process. It identifies the nature of the proceeding and outlines facts to support the complainants' request that the case be decided in his/her favor.

constructive abandonment. A parent who has regular contact with his/her minor child yet willfully and intentionally refuses to consistently fulfill his/her duties and responsibilities as a parent could be held to have constructively abandoned his/her child. Constructive abandonment is a form of neglect.

custodial parent. Generally refers to the parent who either by consent or court order has custody of the minor child.

custody. Refers to the control or authority exercised by a parent over his/her minor child.

D

defendant. The person who is being sued.

diligent search. Before a party can be served with a complaint by publishing a notice in a newspaper, the plaintiff must engage in a diligent search for his/her whereabouts.

divided custody. A custody arrangement in which both parents have primary physical custody of at least one of the parents' children and the parents do not share custody of any of the children.

DNA testing. The most common paternity test uses DNA or genetic traits to determine whether a given man could be the biological father of a given child.

E

emancipation. A court action in which a parent's rights or authority is relinquished. Minor children who are married, enlisted in the military or self-supporting can petition the court to be emancipated.

expert witness. A witness having a special knowledge of the subject about which he/she is to testify. Psychiatrists and child psychologists are examples of expert witnesses.

extraordinary expenses. Expenses incurred by a minor child that are not usual or customary. These expenses are taken into account when calculating child support. The court determines whether or not an expense is extraordinary.

F

financial affidavit. A sworn statement, which includes information about the party's income, expenses, what they own and what they owe. The information is used to calculate child support and to satisfy the court that the party seeking custody is able to support the minor child.

G

genetic sampling. See *DNA testing.*

gross income. A party's income before any taxes or other items are deducted. Gross income is used to calculate a non-custodial parents child support obligation.

guardian *ad litem*. A person appointed by the court to advocate on behalf of the best interests of the minor child in a termination of parental rights action.

H

hearsay rule. A rule which prohibits a witness from testifying about statements made by someone who is not a party to the proceeding. The hearsay rule is designed to ensure the integrity of the testimony presented in court.

home studies. A report prepared by social workers after visiting the parties homes and observing how the child interacts with each parent. The report is used by the court to make a determination about custody. Home studies are also used in adoption cases.

I

imputed income. It is the income a parent has the potential to receive if he/she were to obtain employment in a field that is compatible with his/her education, training, experience or background.

income. The amount of money a person receives from the following sources: salaries, wages, commissions, bonuses, dividends, severance pay, pensions, interest, annuities, capital gains, social security, workers compensation, unemployment insurance, disability pay, gifts or prizes.

interested person. A person with a "legitimate interest" in a minor child's well being and therefore has standing to initiate a custody or termination of parental rights action against a natural parent(s).

J

joint custody. A situation where both parents share responsibility for decision making and physical custody of a minor child.

joint managing conservatorship. In some states, Texas for example, it is the phrase used to describe a joint custody arrangement.

L

legal custody. A parent who has the authority to make decisions on behalf of his/her minor child regarding matters such as medical treatment, education and religious training is deemed to have legal custody. It is not unusual for a court to award one parent sole physical custody and allow both parents to have joint legal custody.

legal guardian. An officer or agent of the court who is appointed to protect the interests of minor children and to provide for their care, welfare, education, maintenance and support.

M

material change of circumstances. See *significant change of circumstances.*

maternal preference. A preference some judges have to keep children in their "tender years" with their mother. This is not the law in most states.

mediation. An intervention, ordered by the court in custody disputes, to promote reconciliation, settlement and compromise between the parties. In many states, mediation is mandatory. In these jurisdictions, the judge can not hear a case until after the party's have participated in mediation.

minor child. A child who has not yet reached the age of majority. The age of majority in most states is 18 years old.

motion. A document which is filed with the court when the parties already have an open case. Motions follow the same format as a petition or complaint. A party files a motion to ask the court to order the opposing party to take or refrain from a specific action.

N

natural parents. See *biological parents.*

neglect. The failure and willful indifference of a parent in the fulfillment of his/her duties and responsibilities for the care and maintenance of his/her minor child. Neglect is grounds for termination of parental rights.

non-custodial parent. A parent who does not share a residence with his/her minor child.

P

parens patriae. A Latin term which relates to the concept of standing often used by divorce courts when acting on behalf of the state to protect and control the property and custody of minor children.

parental liability. The responsibility a parent has for the torts or the wrongful acts committed by his/her minor children. Most states have laws which limit the dollar amount of a parent's liability.

parenting plan. A plan created by parents' that outlines the custody arrangement they feel is in their minor child's best interest. The plan is filed with the court and used by the judge in making custody determinations.

paternity. The state of being a father.

paternity action. A civil lawsuit that a person files to ask a court to determine whether a given man could be the biological father of a given child.

paternity affidavit. A written statement signed before a notary or other official, in which the father acknowledges paternity. The affidavit must also be signed by the mother.

petition. See *complaint.*

petitioner. See *complainant.*

physical abandonment. A parent who chooses not to have physical contact and to separate himself or herself from his/her minor child for an extended period of time (usually six months or longer) is deemed to have physically abandoned the child. In most states, incarceration is not considered to be the equivalent of physical abandonment.

physical custody. In a custody arrangement, the parent with whom a minor child resides is deemed to have physical custody.

physical placement. The term some states, Wisconsin for example, use to describe where a minor child resides.

plaintiff. See *complainant.*

preponderance of the evidence. The traditional standard of proof in civil cases. In a custody case for example, the party whose evidence is more convincing will prevail.

primary caretaker. The parent who provides for the minor child's day-to-day care. The primary caretaker often has an advantage in custody disputes.

primary custody. In joint custody arrangements, the parent with whom the child resides for the majority of days each year is said to have primary custody.

putative father. The man alleged to have fathered the child whose parentage is at issue in a paternity suit.

R

relevancy. The facts and evidence a party presents at trial must relate to the case at hand. Evidence will be deemed relevant if it has a tendency to prove a fact in issue.

respondent. See *defendant.*

S

secondary custody. In joint custody arrangements, the parent with whom the child does not spend the majority of days each year is said to have secondary custody. A parent who has been awarded visitation might also be deemed to have secondary custody.

shared custody. See *joint custody.*

shared parental responsibility. The term some states, Florida for example, use to describe joint custody.

sole custody. The term used to describe situations where one parent is awarded both physical and legal custody.

standing. The law only allows certain people to initiate lawsuits. Such persons are said to have standing. State statutes outline who is allowed or has standing to file paternity, custody, visitation or child support actions.

statutes. The set of volumes that contain the laws passed by a state's legislature. Also referred to as codes.

summons. A form, usually available from the clerk of court, that must be delivered to the person being sued. The summons, which is attached to the complaint, puts the defendant on notice that he/she must file some kind of response to the complaint within a certain number of days, and that if a response is not filed he/she may lose the case by default.

supervised visitation. Visitation that must take place under the direct supervision of someone selected by the court. Such supervision is ordered by the court based on the judge's conclusion that the visiting parent poses a threat to the child if not supervised.

status quo. The condition or situation that existed at the time a court action is commenced. In custody disputes, courts are reluctant to disrupt the status quo or remove a minor child from a place where he or she is thriving and developing normally.

T

termination of parental rights. A court action that severs all legal ties between the parent and the minor child. It is considered to be one of the most severe court actions that can be brought against a parent.

third party custody. When the court awards someone other than a natural parent, a grandparent for example, custody of a minor child.

third party visitation. Where the court awards someone other than the non-custodial parent, a grandparent for example, visitation with a minor child.

U

unfit parent. A parent who is incompetent or unsuitable to have the care or control of his/her minor child(ren). Unfitness generally relates to some type of moral delinquency.

Uniform Child Custody Jurisdiction Act (UCCJA). A law that dictates that a court can not enter or modify a court order until the minor child has resided in the state for at least six months and the court is made aware of any prior or pending custody disputes and the names of any person who is not a party to the legal action but has a legal claim to the minor child.

Uniform Child Custody Jurisdiction Affidavit. The affidavit containing the information required by the UCCJA. It must be attached to all custody and visitation complaints.

Uniform Interstate Family Support Act. A federal law that requires states to cooperate in the collection of child support. It ensures there is only one valid support order to enforce when more than one state is involved in a case.

V

verification. A sworn statement in which a party declares that all of the information included in the complaint is true, either because he/she knows first hand that it is true or because he/she believes it to be true.

visitation. The opportunity the court grants to non-custodial parents to visit with a minor child on a prescribed schedule.

W

witness. A person who testifies in a court proceeding.

APPENDIX A:
STATE-BY-STATE LAWS

This appendix contains an alphabetical listing of the fifty states and the District of Columbia. Each state's listing includes basic information which should assist you in preparing your legal forms and finding any additional information you may need. (The abbreviation "Sec." means section.)

The Law	This listing provides the name of the set of books which contain the state's laws, and an example of how they are divided into sections, chapters, articles, etc. For example, under the listing for Alabama you find the following notation:
The Law	Code of Alabama. ***Example***: Code of Alabama, Title 30, Chapter 2, Section 30-2-1 (C.A. sec. 30-2-1).

This tells you that "Code of Alabama" is the title of the books containing the laws of Alabama. It also tells you that the books are subdivided into titles, chapters, and sections. "Code of Alabama, Title 30, Chapter 2, Section 30-2-1" is abbreviated "C.A. Sec. 30-2-1." You will often find that the section number incorporates the number of the title, chapter, article, etc. Ask the librarian to assist you in locating the volume which contains the laws governing the kind of case in which you are involved.

Case Style

This provides an example of the heading that should be placed at the beginning of any legal forms you file. You should verify the accuracy of the case style by reviewing a case file at the courthouse. If the case style used in the case file is different from the example included in this appendix, use the format your find in the case file.

Designation of Parties

This tells you how you and the opposing party should be designated in court papers. This will either be *Plaintiff* and *Defendant*, or *Petitioner* and *Respondent*.

Custody

This provides a general summary of the factors a court will consider in determining custody.

Child Support

This provides a general summary of the state's child support laws. If your state has child support guidelines, contact the court clerk's office at the courthouse about where you can obtain a copy. They usually include instructions on how to use the guidelines. This section will also indicate the age at which the child support obligation normally ends. (However, keep in mind that there may be extenuating factors which may extend a parent's obligation beyond the age cited in this listing.)

Termination of Parental Rights

This provides a general summary of the state's grounds for the termination of parental rights.

Alabama

The Law

Code of Alabama. ***Example***: Code of Alabama, Title 30, Chapter 2, Section 30-2-1 (C.A. Sec. 30-2-1).

Case Style

IN THE CIRCUIT COURT FOR _____COUNTY, ALABAMA

Designation
of Parties

_____, Plaintiff, and
_____, Defendant.

Custody

Factors: (1) moral character of parents; and (2) age and sex of child. Joint custody possible.

Child Support

Either parent may be ordered to pay, "as may seem right and proper, having regard to the moral character and prudence of the parents and age and sex of children." Termination age: 19.

Termination of
Parental Rights

Grounds: (1) abandonment; (2) emotional or mental illness or mental deficiency of parent; (3) excessive substance abuse by parent; (4) child abused or in danger of abuse by parent; (5) physical injury of child resulting from neglect; and (6) parent convicted and imprisoned for a felony.

Alaska

The Law	Alaska Statutes. ***Example***: Alaska Statutes, Title 25, Section 25.24.010 (A.S. Sec. 25.24.010).
Case Style	SUPERIOR COURT FOR THE STATE OF ALASKA # _____ JUDICIAL DISTRICT
Designation of Parties	_____Petitioner, vs. _____, Respondent.
Custody	Factors: Best interest of the child considering: (1)physical, emotional, mental, religious, and social needs of the child; (2) capability and desire of each party to meet those needs; (3) child's preference, if of suitable age and ability; (4) love and affection existing between each child and each party; (5) length of time the child has been in a stable, satisfactory environment, and the desirability of maintaining continuity; (6) desire and ability of each party to allow an open and loving frequent relationship between the child and the other party;

(continued)

Custody (cont.)

(7) any evidence of domestic violence, child abuse or neglect in the proposed custodial home, or history of violence between the parties; (8) any evidence that substance abuse by either party or other household member directly affects the child's emotional or physical well-being; (9) any other relevant factor.

Child Support

Factors: (1) child's needs; (2) ability of both parties to meet those needs; (3) extent of support by the parent during the marriage; (4) economic ability of each party to pay. Termination age: 18.

Termination of Parental Rights

Grounds: (1) parent without custody unreasonably withholds consent to adoption; and (2) child was conceived as a result of sexual abuse of a minor.

Arizona

The Law	Arizona Revised Statutes.
	Example: Arizona Revised Statutes, Section 25-311 (A.R.S. Sec. 25-311).
Case Style	IN THE SUPERIOR COURT OF THE STATE OF ARIZONA
	IN AND FOR THE COUNTY OF
	_____
Designation of Parties	_____ Petitioner, and
	_____, Respondent.
Custody	Factors: Best interest of the child considering: (1) parties' wishes; (2) child's wishes; (3) interaction and interrelationship between the child and each parent, siblings and other significant persons; (4) child's adjustment to home, school, and community; (5) mental and physical health of all persons involved; (6) which parent is more likely to allow frequent and continuing contact with the other parent; (7) whether any parent provided primary care; (8) whether there was any coercion or duress by one parent in obtaining a custody agreement; and (9) whether there was any domestic violence. Joint custody may be granted if the parties agree and submit a written joint custody agreement.

(continued)

Child Support

State child support guidelines available from court clerk. Termination age: 18.

Termination of
Parental Rights

Grounds: (1) abandonment; (2) neglect or willful abuse of the child; (3) mental illness or mental deficiency of parent or chronic substance abuse by parent; (4) parent convicted and incarcerated for a felony of such as to prove parent unfit; (5) potential father failed to file paternity action within 30 days as prescribed by law; and (6) parents relinquished rights to child to an agency or consented to adoption.

Arkansas

The Law	Arkansas Code of 1987 Annotated. ***Example***: Arkansas Code Annotated, Title 9, Chapter 12, Section 9-12-301 (A.C.A. Sec. 9-12-301).
Case Style	IN THE CHANCERY COURT OF _____ ARKANSAS
Designation of Parties	_____, Plaintiff vs. _____, Defendant.
Custody	Only statutory provision is that custody be determined "without regard to the sex of the parent but solely in accordance with the welfare and best interest of the child."
Child Support	Arkansas Family Support guidelines chart is available from Chancery Court Clerk. Termination age: 18.
Termination of Parental Rights	Grounds: 1) abandonment; (2) neglect or abuse; and (3) parent without custody unreasonably withholds consent to adoption.

California

The Law	West's Annotated California Codes. ***Example***: Family Code, Section 2300. (California has several Annotated California Codes, such as the Family Code, Probate Code, etc. Ask the librarian if you need assistance.)
Case Style	SUPERIOR COURT OF CALIFORNIA, COUNTY OF _____.
Designation of Parties	_____Petitioner, vs. _____Respondent.
Custody	Factors: (1) child's health, safety and welfare; (2) any history of abuse; (3) nature and amount of contact with each parent; and (4) any other factor the court considers relevant. Marital misconduct may be considered.
Child Support	State child support guidelines available from court clerk. Termination age: 18.
Termination of Parental Rights	Grounds: (1) abandonment; (2) neglect or abuse of the child; (3) substance abuse by parent; (4) parent convicted of a felony; (5) emotional or mental illness or mental deficiency of parent; and (6) out of home placement of child for over one year.

Colorado

The Law	West's Colorado Revised Statutes Annotated. ***Example***: Colorado Revised Statutes Annotated, Title 14, Article 10, Section 14-10-106 (C.R.S.A. Sec. 14-10-106).
Case Style	IN THE DISTRICT COURT IN AND FOR THE COUNTY OF _____ AND STATE OF COLORADO
Designation of Parties	_____, Petitioner, vs. _____ Respondent.
Custody	Factors: Best interest of the child, considering: (1) parties' wishes; (2) child's wishes; (3) interaction and interrelationship between the child and the parties, siblings and other significant persons; (4) child's adjustment to home, school and community; (5) mental and physical health of all persons involved; (6) custodian's ability to encourage sharing, love, affection and contact with the other party; (7) evidence of the parties ability to cooperate and make joint decisions;

(continued)

Custody (cont.)

(8) evidence of each party's ability to encourage sharing, love, affection and contact with the other party; (9) whether the past pattern of involvement of the parties with the child reflects a system of values, time commitment, and mutual support which would indicate an ability as joint custodians to provide a positive and nourishing relationship with the child; (10) physical proximity of the parties as it relates to practical considerations of awarding joint custody; (11) whether joint custody will promote more frequent or continuing contacts; (12) any history of child abuse or neglect; and (13) any history of spouse abuse.

Child Support

State child support guidelines and tables are found in C.R.S.A. Sec. 14-10-115. Termination age: 21.

Termination of Parental Rights

Grounds: (1) emotional or mental illness or mental deficiency of parent; (2) physical or sexual abuse of the child by the parent; (3) violent behavior of parent; (4) substance abuse by the parent; and (5) neglect of the child by the parent.

Connecticut

The Law	Connecticut General Statutes Annotated. ***Example***: Connecticut General Statutes Annotated, Title 46b, Section 46b-40 (C.G.S.A. Sec. 46b-40). Ignore "chapter" numbers.
Case Style	IN THE SUPERIOR COURT OF THE STATE OF CONNECTICUT
Designation of Parties	_____ Plaintiff, vs. _____, Defendant
Custody	Best interest of the child considering wishes of the child, if sufficient age. Law favors joint custody if both parties agree.
Child Support	Factors: (1) age, health, station, occupation, earning capacity, amount and sources of income, estate, vocational skills and employability of the parties; (2) child's age, health, station, occupation, educational status and expectation, amount and sources of income, vocational skills, employability, estate and needs. Termination age: 18.
Termination of Parental Rights	Grounds: (1) abandonment; and (2) neglect.

Delaware

The Law	Delaware Code Annotated. ***Example***: Delaware Code Annotated, Title 13, Section 1502 (D.C.A. 13 Sec. 1502).
Case Style	IN THE FAMILY COURT OF THE STATE OF DELAWARE IN AND FOR _____ COUNTY
Designation of Parties	_____ Petitioner vs. _____, Respondent.
Custody	Determined by the best interest of the child, considering: (1) wishes of the parents and the child, (2) interaction and interrelationship of the child with parents, siblings, and other significant persons; (3) child's adjustment to home, school and community; and (4) mental and physical health of all persons involved.
Child Support	Factors: (1) health, relative economic condition, financial circumstances and income of the parties and child; (2) general equities inherent in the situation. Formula and forms may be found in Family Court Civil Rules, Rule 52(c) and Forms 509 and 509p. Termination age: 18.

(continued)

Termination of
Parental Rights

Grounds: (1) abandonment; (2) parents are mentally incompetent; (3) parent convicted of a felony in which child was a victim or involved harm to child; and (4) parents unable or failed to provide for physical, mental or emotional welfare of child.

District of Columbia

The Law

District of Columbia Code. **Example**: District of Columbia Code, Title 16, Section 901 (D.C.C. Sec. 16-901).

Case Style

IN THE SUPERIOR COURT OF THE DISTRICT OF COLUMBIA - FAMILY DIVISION

Designation
of Parties

_____ Plaintiff vs.
_____, Defendant.

Custody

Best interest of the child considering: (1) wishes of the child; (2) wishes of the parties; (3) the interaction and interrelationship between the child and parents, siblings and other significant persons; (4) child's adjustment to home, school and community; and (5) mental and physical health of all persons involved.

Child Support

State child support guidelines found in D.C.C. Sec. 16-916.1.
Termination age: 18.

Termination of
Parental Rights

Grounds: (1) physical, mental and emotional health of parent which affect the child's welfare; and (2) substance abuse by parent.

Florida

The Law	Florida Statutes. ***Example***: Florida Statutes, Chapter 61, Section 61.001 (F.S. Sec. 61.001). A new set of statute books is published in odd-numbered year, and supplemental volumes even-numbered year. You may also find West's Florida Statutes Annotated, with pocket part supplements. Most current changes are found in soft-cover volumes of Florida Session Laws, published at the end of each legislative session. Florida has many official forms, found in the Florida Rules of Court, or obtained from the court clerk.
Case Style	IN THE CIRCUIT COURT OF THE____JUDICIAL [Each circuit has a number] CIRCUIT, IN AND FOR _____ COUNTY, FLORIDA
Designation of Parties	_____, Petitioner vs. _____, Respondent
Custody	Joint custody (referred to as "joint parental responsibility") is preferred, and must be ordered unless judge finds it would be detrimental to the child. Generally this refers to joint responsibility for making decisions for the child's welfare, with one party's home being designated as the "primary residence." Responsibility and primary residence determined by the best interest of the child considering:

(continued)

Custody (cont.)

(1) which party is more likely to allow frequent and continuing contact with the other party; (2) love, affection and other emotional ties existing between the child and each party; (3) each party's capacity and disposition to provide food, clothing, medical care or other material needs for the child; (4) length of time the child has been in a stable, satisfactory environment, and the desirability of maintaining continuity; (5) the permanence, as a family unit, of the existing or proposed custodial home; (6) moral fitness of the parties; (7) mental and physical health of the parties; (8) child's home, school and community record; (9) preference of the child, if sufficient intelligence, understanding and experience; and (10) any other relevant factor.

Child Support

State child support guidelines may be found in F.S. Sec. 61.30.
Termination age: 18.

Termination of
Parental Rights

Grounds: (1) abandonment; (2) conduct of parent which threatens life or well-being of the child; (3) parent is incarcerated in state or federal prison; and (4) parent engages in egregious conduct which threatens health or safety of child.

Georgia

The Law	Official Code of Georgia Annotated. ***Example***: Official Code of Georgia Annotated, Title 19, Chapter 5, Section 1 (C.G.A. Sec. 19-5-1).
Case Style	IN THE SUPERIOR COURT OF _____ GEORGIA
Designation of Parties	_____, Petitioner vs. _____ Respondent
Custody	No specific factors or provisions for joint custody in statute. Child may select parent to live with if at least 14 years of age.
Child Support	Basically figured as a percent of the payor's gross income, as follows: 17% to 23% for one child; 23% to 28% for two children; 25% to 32% for three children; 29% to 35% for four children; and 31% to 37% for five or more children. This can be modified by special circumstances. Guidelines found at C.G.A. Sec. 19-6-15. Termination age: 18.

(continued)

Termination of
Parental Rights

Grounds: (1) abandonment; (2) mental, physical and emotional health which renders parent unable to care for child; (3) excessive use of alcohol or drugs; (4) conviction of a felony which adversely affects parent/child relationship; (5) physical, mental or emotional neglect of child; (6) egregious conduct of parent toward the child; and (7) death of a sibling which constitutes evidence that death resulted from neglect or abuse by parent.

Hawaii

The Law	Hawaii Revised Statutes. ***Example***: Hawaii Revised Statutes, Title 580, Section 580-41 (H.R.S. Sec. 580-41).
Case Style	IN THE FAMILY COURT OF THE _____ JUDICIAL CIRCUIT
Designation of Parties	_____, Plaintiff vs. _____, Defendant.
Custody	Best interest of the child considering: (1) child's wishes, if of sufficient age and capacity to reason; and (2) any evidence of family violence.
Child Support	State child support guidelines found at H.R.S. Sec. 576D-7. Termination age: 18.
Termination of Parental Rights	Grounds: Abandonment.

Idaho

The Law	Idaho Code. **Example**: Idaho Code, Title 32, Chapter 6, Section 32-601 (I.C. Sec. 32-601).
Case Style	IN THE DISTRICT COURT OF THE _____ JUDICIAL DISTRICT FOR THE STATE OF IDAHO, IN AND FOR THE COUNTY OF _____.
Designation of Parties	_____ Plaintiff vs. _____ Defendant.
Custody	Best interest of the child considering: (1) wishes of parties; (2) wishes of child; (3) interaction and interrelationship between the child and parties, siblings or other significant persons; (4) adjustment to home, school and community; (5) mental and physical health of all persons involved; (6) need to promote continuity and stability in the child's life; and (7) any history of domestic violence. Joint custody is presumed best, unless either party can show otherwise.
Child Support	State child support guidelines issued by Idaho Supreme Court (obtain from court clerk or law library). Termination age: 18.
Termination of Parental Rights	Grounds: (1) abandonment; (2) neglect or abuse of child by parent; and (3) mental illness or mental deficiency of parent.

Illinois

The Law   West's Smith-Hurd Illinois Compiled Statutes Annotated. **Example**: Illinois Compiled Statutes, Chapter 750, Act 5, Section 5/101 (750 ILCS 5/101).

Case Style   IN THE CIRCUIT COURT OF THE _____ JUDICIAL DISTRICT, _____ COUNTY, ILLINOIS

Designation   _____ Petitioner vs.
of Parties   _____ Respondent

Custody   Factors: (1) wishes of parents and child; (2) interaction and interrelationship between the child and the parents, siblings and other significant persons; (3) child's adjustment to home, school and community; (4) mental and physical health of parties and child; (5) any physical threat to child; and (6) each party's willingness to encourage and facilitate continued contact between the other parent and the child.

Child Support   Basically a percentage of the payor's net income, as follows: 20% for one child; 25% for two children; 32% for three children; 40% for four children; 45% for five children; and 50% for six or more children. Other factors for special needs are listed which may justify more or less. Guidelines found at 750 ILCS 5/505. Termination age: 18.

Termination of   Grounds: Abuse.
Parental Rights

Indiana

The Law

West's Annotated Indiana Code. **Example**: Annotated Indiana Code, Title 31, Article3 1, Chapter 11.5, Section 1 (A.I.C. Sec. 31-1-11.5-1).

Case Style

_____COURT OF _____ COUNTY, INDIANA. The first blank will either be "SUPERIOR," "CIRCUIT," or "DOMESTIC RELATIONS," depending upon the particular county you file in.]

Designation of Parties

_____ Petitioner vs. _____ Respondent

Custody

Factors: (1) age and sex of the child; (2) wishes of the parents and child; (3) interaction and interrelationship between the child and the parents, siblings and other significant persons; (4) child's adjustment to home, school and community; and (5) mental and physical health of all persons involved. Joint legal custody may be awarded.

Child Support

Factors: (1) financial resources of custodial parent; (2) physical and mental condition of the child and the child's educational needs; (3) financial resources and needs of the non]custodial parent; and (4) any special educational or medical needs of the child. Termination age: 18.

(continued)

Termination of
Parental Rights

Grounds: (1) abandonment; (2) parent judicially declared incompetent or mentally defective; and (3) best interest of the child.

Iowa

The Law

Iowa Code Annotated. **Example**: Iowa Code Annotated, Section 598.1 (I.C.A. Sec. 598.1).

Case Style

IN THE DISTRICT COURT OF THE STATE OF IOWA IN AND FOR _____ COUNTY

Designation
of Parties

_____ Petitioner vs.
_____ Respondent.

Custody

Best interest of the child "which will assure the child opportunity for the maximum continuing physical and emotional contact with both parents." Either party may request joint legal custody. If the judge refuses, findings must be in decree, considering various factors in the statute.

Child Support

State child support guidelines found at I.C.A. Sec. 598.21. Termination age: 18.

Termination of
Parental Rights

Grounds: (1) abandonment; (2) abuse or neglect of child; (3) parent imprisoned for crime against the child; (4) parent has a chronic mental illness and presents a danger to self and others; and (5) substance abuse.

Kansas

The Law	Kansas Statutes Annotated. ***Example***: Kansas Statutes Annotated, Section 60-1601 (K.S.A. Sec. 60-1601). You may find these volumes as either "Vernon's Kansas Statutes Annotated," or "Kansas Statutes Annotated, Official." Both sets have very poor indexes.

Case Style

IN THE DISTRICT COURT IN AND FOR THE COUNTY OF _____, KANSAS

Designation
of Parties

_____, Petitioner vs.
_____, Respondent

Custody

Best interest of the child considering: (1) any agreement of the parties; (2) length of time child has been under actual care and control of any person other than a parent and the circumstances involved; (3) desires of the parties; (4) desires of the child; (5) interaction and interrelationship between child and parties, siblings and other significant persons; (6) child's adjustment to home, school and community; (7) each party's willingness and ability to respect and appreciate the bond between the child and the other party; (8) any evidence of spousal abuse; and (9) any other relevant factor.

(continued)

Child Support

Supreme Court Child Support Guidelines may be obtained from court clerk or law library. Termination age: 18.

Termination of Parental Rights

Grounds: (1) emotional or mental illness, mental deficiency of physical disability of parent; (2) physical, emotional or sexual abuse of child; (3) substance abuse; (4) physical, mental or emotional neglect of child; (5) conviction of a felony and imprisonment; and (6) unexplained injury or death of another child of the parent.

Kentucky

The Law

Kentucky Revised Statutes. ***Example***: Kentucky Revised Statutes, Chapter 403, Section 010 (K.R.S. Sec. 403.010).

Case Style

_____ CIRCUIT COURT, KENTUCKY [County name goes in blank]

Designation of Parties

_____ Petitioner, vs. _____ Respondent

Custody

Best interest of the child, considering: (1) wishes of the parents and child; (2) interaction and interrelationship between the child and parents, siblings and other significant persons; (3) child's adjustment to home, school and community; and (4) mental and physical condition of all persons involved. Judge may grant joint custody in the child's best interest.

Child Support

State child support guidelines found at K.R.S. Sec. 403.212. Termination age: 18.

Termination of Parental Rights

Grounds: (1) abandonment; (2) physical or emotional abuse of the child; (3) sexual abuse of the child; (4) failure or inability to provide parental care and protection; and (5) failure to provide food, clothes, and shelter for the child for reasons other than poverty.

Louisiana

The Law	West's Louisiana Statutes Annotated. Some will be titled with the abbreviation "LSA." The books containing the laws of Louisiana are one of the more complicated sets of any state. They are divided into subjects, so you need to be sure you have the properly labeled set, such as "Civil Code," "Revised Statutes," or "Code of Civil Procedure." **Example**: LSA Civil Code, Article 102 (C.C., Art. 102). Ask the law librarian if you need assistance.

Case Style

_____ JUDICIAL DISTRICT COURT, PARISH OF _____,
LOUISIANA
[District number goes in first blank]

Designation of Parties

_____ Plaintiff vs.
_____ Defendant

Custody

Joint legal custody is preferred and presumed best for the child. Parties must submit a joint custody plan. If one party requests sole custody, he or she must prove it is in the child's best interest considering the following factors: (1) the child's love, affection and emotional ties with each parent; (2) capacity and disposition of the parties to give love, affection, guidance, education and religious guidance; (3) capacity and disposition of the parties to give the child food, clothing and medical care, etc.,

(continued)

Custody (cont.)

(4) length of time the child has been in a stable, satisfactory environment, and the desirability for continuity; (5) permanence as a family unit for existing or proposed home; (6) moral fitness of the parties; (7) mental and physical health of the parties; (8) home, school and community record of the child; (9) preference of the child, if the child is of sufficient age; (10) willingness of each party to facilitate a relationship between the child and the opposing party; (11) distances between the parties residences; and (12) any other factor the judge decides is proper.

Child Support

Based upon (1) needs of the child; and (2) actual resources of each parent. Guidelines found in LSA Revised Statutes, 9:315. Termination age: 18.

Termination of Parental Rights

Grounds: (1) misconduct of parent toward the child which constitutes extreme abuse, cruel and inhuman treatment or grossly neglectful behavior; (2) abuse or neglect which is life threatening; and (3) abandonment.

Maine

The Law

Page's Maine Revised Statutes Annotated.
Example: Maine Revised Statutes Annotated, Title 19, Section 661 (19 M.R.S.A. Sec. 661).

Case Style

STATE OF MAINE, _____
COURT   _____
COUNTY
[First blank is for either "DISTRICT" or "SUPERIOR"]

Designation
of Parties

_____, Plaintiff vs.
_____, Defendant

Custody

Best interest of child considering: (1) child's age; (2) child's relationship with each party and other significant persons; (3) preference of child, if suitable age and maturity; (4) duration and adequacy of child's current living arrangement and desirability of maintaining continuity; (5) stability of proposed living arrangement; (6) motivation of the parties and their capacity to give love, affection and guidance; (7) child's adjustment to home, school and community;

(continued)

Custody (cont.)

(8) each party's capacity to allow and encourage a relationship between the child and the other party; (9) each party's capacity to cooperate in child care; (10) the methods of assisting parental cooperation and resolving disputes and each party's willingness to use those methods; (11) effect on the child if one party has sole authority regarding upbringing; (12) any history of domestic abuse; and (13) any other relevant factor.

Child Support

State child support guidelines available from court clerk. Termination age: 18.

Termination of Parental Rights

Grounds: (1) abandonment; (2) parent has acted toward a child in a way that is heinous or abhorrent to society; and (3) parent was convicted of a felony where the child was a victim.

Maryland

The Law	Annotated Code of Maryland. ***Example***: Annotated Code of Maryland, Family Law, Section 7-101 (A.C.M., Family Law Sec. 7-101). Volumes are arranged by subject, so be sure you have the correctly titled volume.
Case Style	IN THE CIRCUIT COURT FOR _____ COUNTY, MARYLAND
Designation of Parties	_____, Plaintiff vs. _____, Defendant.
Custody	There are no statutory factors.
Child Support	State child support guidelines and table found in A.C.M., Family Law Secs. 12-201 and 12-204. Termination age: 18.
Termination of Parental Rights	Grounds: (1) child has been out of the custody of the natural parents for over one year; (2) parent has been convicted of child abuse; and (3) parent has been convicted of a crime of violence and imprisoned for at least ten years.

Massachusetts

The Law	Annotated Laws of Massachusetts. ***Example***: Annotated Laws of Massachusetts, Chapter 208, Section 1 (A.L.M., C208, Sec. 1).
Case Style	COMMONWEALTH OF MASSACHUSETTS, _____ COURT
Designation of Parties	_____ Plaintiff vs. _____ Defendant
Custody	No factors in statute; only general concepts including best interests of the child.
Child Support	State child support guidelines available from court clerk. Termination age: 18.
Termination of Parental Rights	Grounds: (1) abandonment; (2) child or sibling abused or neglected by parent; (3) parent fails to provide child proper care or custody; (4) severe or repetitive conduct toward the child of a physically, emotionally or sexually abusive or neglectful nature; and (5) felony conviction of parent.

Michigan

The Law
Michigan Statutes Annotated (M.S.A.) or Michigan Compiled Laws Annotated (M.C.L.A). Michigan has two official sets of laws, each from a different publisher. ***Example***: M.S.A. Sec. 25.96(1) or M.C.L.A. Sec. 552.16a.

Case Style
STATE OF MICHIGAN _____
JUDICIAL   CIRCUIT,   _____
COUNTY
[Circuit number in first blank]

Designation
of Parties
_____, Complainant vs.
_____ Defendant

Custody
Best interest of child, considering the following factors: (1) love, affection and other emotional ties existing between the parties and the child; (2) the capacity and disposition of each to give love, affection, guidance and continuation of education and raising the child in its religion; (3) the capacity and disposition of each to provide food, clothing and medical care; (4) length of time the child has lived in a stable, satisfactory environment and the desirability of maintaining continuity;

(continued)

Custody (cont.)

(5) permanence as a family unit of the existing or proposed custodial home; (6) moral fitness of the parties; (7) mental and physical health of the parties and the child; (8) home, school and community record of the child; (9) preference of the child, if of suitable age; (10) willingness and ability of the parties to facilitate and encourage a relationship between the child and the other parent; and (11) any other relevant factor. Joint custody may be considered.

Child Support

Child support may continue beyond age of 18 if the child is regularly attending high school on a full-time basis, with a reasonable expectation of graduating while residing with the custodial parent; but in no event beyond the age of 19 years, 6 months. Termination age: 18.

Termination of Parental Rights

Grounds: (1) abandonment; (2) physical injury, physical or sexual abuse by parent; (3) parent fails to provide proper care or custody for the child; (4) parent imprisoned for such a period that child will be deprived of normal home life; (5) parental rights terminated due to serious and chronic neglect or abuse; and (6) child will be harmed if returned to parent.

Minnesota

The Law	Minnesota Statutes Annotated. ***Example***: Minnesota Statutes Annotated, Section 518.002 (M.S.A. Sec. 518.002).
Case Style	STATE OF MINNESOTA DISTRICT COURT COUNTY OF _____, _____ JUDICIAL DISTRICT
Designation of Parties	_____ Petitioner vs. _____ Respondent
Custody	Factors: (1) the parties' wishes; (2) child's preference, if of sufficient age; (3) child's primary caretaker; (4) intimacy of the relationship between child and each party; (5) interaction and interrelationship between child and the parties, siblings and other significant persons; (6) child's adjustment to home, school and community; (7) length of time in a stable, satisfactory environment and desirability of maintaining continuity; (8) permanence, as a family unit, of the existing or proposed home; (9) mental and physical health of all persons involved;

(continued)

Custody (cont.)

(10) each party's capacity and disposition to give love, affection and guidance and to continue educating and raising the child in the child's culture and religion, if any; (11) child's cultural background; (12) effect of any domestic violence on the child; and (13) any other relevant factor. Additional considerations where joint custody is requested. See M.S.A. Sec. 518.179 for list of criminal acts that will prohibit an award of custody.

Child Support

State child support guidelines found in M.S.A. Sec. 518.551.
Termination age: 18.

Termination of Parental Rights

Grounds: (1) abandonment; (2) parent refused or neglected to comply with duties imposed upon a parent; (3) parent is palpably unfit to be a party to the parent/child relationship; (4) child adjudicated in need of protection; (5) parental rights as one or more children involuntarily terminated; (6) parent diagnosed as chemically dependent; (7) child experienced severe harm in parent's care; and (8) child placed in foster care due to parental neglect.

Mississippi

The Law	Mississippi Code 1972 Annotated. ***Example***: Mississippi Code, Section 93-5-1 (M.C. Sec. 93-5-1).
Case Style	CHANCERY COURT OF _____ COUNTY, STATE OF MISSISSIPPI
Designation of Parties	_____, COMPLAINANT vs. _____ DEFENDANT
Custody	No statutory factors. Child may choose if at least age 12. Presumption in favor of joint custody, both physical and decision making. Judge may require custody plan from parties.
Child Support	No statutory factors. Generally, child support is determined by the relative and proportionate incomes and abilities of the parties. Termination age: 21.
Termination of Parental Rights	Grounds: (1) abandonment; (2) parent responsible for series of abusive incidents concerning the child; (3) substance abuse by the parent; (4) parent suffers from severe mental deficiencies or mental illness; and (5) parent convicted of physical or sexual abuse against child.

Missouri

The Law	Vernon's Annotated Missouri Statutes **Example**: Annotated Missouri Statutes, Chapter 452, Section 452.300 (A.M.S. Sec. 452.300).
Case Style	IN THE CIRCUIT COURT_____ COUNTY, MISSOURI
Designation of Parties	_____ Petitioner vs. _____ Respondent
Custody	Best interest of the child considering: (1) wishes of the parties; (2) wishes of the child; (3) interaction and interrelationship between child and parties, siblings and other significant persons; (4) child's adjustment to home, school and community; (5) mental and physical health, and any abuse history, of all persons involved; (6) child's needs for continuing relationship with both parties, and the ability and willingness of each to actively perform their duties as mother and father for the needs of the child; (7) any intention of either party to relocate outside the state; (8) which party is more likely to allow frequent and meaningful contact between the child and the other party; and (9) any other relevant factor.

(continued)

Child Support

Factors: (1) financial needs and resources of the child; (2) financial resources and needs of the parties; (3) standard of living child would have had if no divorce ; and (4) child's physical and emotional condition and educational needs.
Termination age: 18.

Termination of Parental Rights

Grounds: (1) abandonment; (2) child has been abused or neglected; (3) parent has been found guilty of a felony violation where child or sibling was victim; (4) child was conceived as a result of rape; and (5) parent unfit because of substance abuse.

Montana

The Law

Montana Code Annotated. **Example**: Montana Code Annotated, Title 40, Chapter 4, Section 40-4-101 (M.C.A. Sec. 40-4-101).

Case Style

DISTRICT COURT FOR THE STATE OF MONTANA AND FOR THE COUNTY OF_____

Designation of Parties

_____ Petitioner vs.

_____ Respondent

Custody

Factors: (1) parties' wishes; (2) child's wishes; (3) interaction and interrelationship between child and parties, siblings, and other significant persons; (4) child's adjustment to home, school and community (5) mental and physical condition of all persons involved; (6) any physical abuse, or threat of physical abuse, against a party or the child; (7) any chemical dependency or abuse of either party; and (8) any other relevant factor. Joint custody may be granted but parties will be required to submit to custody plan.

Child Support

Factors: (1) child' financial resources; (2) custodial parent's financial resources; (3) child's physical and emotional condition and educational and medical needs; (4) noncustodial parent's financial resources and needs; (5) child' age; (6) cost of day care; (7) custody arrangements; and (8) needs of any other person either party is obligated to support.
Termination age: 18.

Termination of Parental Rights

Grounds: (1) parent is unfit; (2) relationship of parent and child doesn't exist; and (3) parent has irrevocably waived parental rights.

Nebraska

The Law	Revised Statutes of Nebraska. *Example*: Revised Statutes of Nebraska, Chapter 42, Article 3, Section 42-301 (R.S.N. Sec. 42-301).

Case Style

IN THE DISTRICT COURT FOR
_____ COUNTY,
NEBRASKA

Designation
of Parties

_____ Petitioner vs.
_____ Respondent

Custody

Best interest of the child considering: (1) the relationship of the child and each party; (2) reasonable desires of the child; and (3) the general health, welfare and social behavior of the child. Shared or joint custody is possible if both parties agree and a hearing shows it is in the best interest of the child.

Child Support

The state's child support guidelines available from court clerk.
Termination age: 19.

Termination of
Parental Rights

Grounds: (1) abandonment; (2) child substantially and continuously neglected by parent; (3) parent neglected to provide child with necessary subsistence; (4) parents are unfit by reason of debauchery, habitual use of alcohol or drugs; and (5) parent is unable to perform responsibilities because of mental illness or deficiency.

Nevada

The Law

Nevada Revised Statutes Annotated. **Example**: Nevada Revised Statutes Annotated, Chapter 125, Section 125.010 (N.R.S.A. Sec. 125.010).

Case Style

IN THE DISTRICT COURT FOR
_____ COUNTY, NEVADA

Designation of Parties

_____ Plaintiff vs.
_____ Defendant

Custody

Best interest of the child considering: (1) which party is more likely to allow frequent association and continuing relationship with the other party; (2) wishes of the child, if of sufficient age and intelligence; (3) "any nomination by a parent of a guardian for the child"; and (4) whether either party has engaged in an act of domestic violence against the child, the other party, or other person residing with the child. Preference is for joint custody.

(continued)

Child Support

Based upon the following percentage of gross income: 18% for one child; 25% for two children; 29% for three children; 31% for four children; and an additional 2% for each additional child. Minimum support of $100 per month per child, unless the judge finds the payor is unable to pay that amount. Any deviation from these percentages, even where the parties agree, must be explained in the decree, by considering: (1) extraordinary needs of the child are not being met; (2) cost of health insurance; (3) cost of child care; (4) special educational needs; (5) age of child; (6) the parties' other support obligations; (7) value of services contributed by either party; (8) any public assistance paid to support the child; (9) expenses reasonably related to pregnancy and confinement; (10) cost of transportation for visitation if custodial parent moved from the jurisdiction of the court; (11) amount of time child spends with each party; (12) other necessary expenses for the child's benefit; and (13) the parties relative income. Termination age: 18.

Termination of Parental Rights

Grounds: (1) abandonment; (2) neglect of the child; (3) unfitness of the parent; (4) failure of parental adjustment; and (5) risk of physical, mental or emotional injury to child if the child remains with the parent.

New Hampshire

The Law	New Hampshire Revised Statutes Annotated. ***Example***: New Hampshire Revised Statutes Annotated, Chapter 458, Section 458:4 (N.H.R.S.A. Sec. 458:4).
Case Style	THE STATE OF NEW HAMPSHIRE, SUPERIOR COURT IN AND FOR _____ COUNTY
Designation of Parties	_____, Petitioner vs. _____, Respondent
Custody	Joint legal custody is presumed in the child's best interest, unless abuse is shown. Final order must state reasons if joint legal custody is not ordered. Factors: (1) preference of the child; and (2) any domestic violence.
Child Support	Needs based on a percentage of the parties' combined net income as follows: 25% for one child; 33% for two children; 40% for three children; and 45% for four or more children. Each party responsible for a pro rate share of the needs according to income. Termination age: 18.

(continued)

Termination of
Parental Rights

Grounds: (1) abandonment; (2) parent has neglected to provide the child with necessary subsistence; (3) child neglect or abuse; (4) mental deficiency or mental illness rendering parent incapable of giving child proper parental care; (5) parent knowingly or willingly caused sexual, physical, emotional or mental abuse of child; and (6) incarceration of parent for a felony.

New Jersey

The Law

NJSA (New Jersey Statutes Annotated).
Example: NJSA, Title 2A, Chapter 34,
Section 2A:34-2 (NJSA Sec. 2A:34-2).

Case Style

SUPERIOR COURT OF NEW JERSEY,
CHANCERY DIVISION,
FAMILY PART, _____
COUNTY

Designation
of Parties

_____ Plaintiff, vs.
_____ Defendant

Custody

Best interest of the child considering the
following factors: (1) parent's ability to
agree, communicate and cooperate in
matters relating to the child; (2) parents'
willingness to accept custody and facilitate visitation; (3) interaction and interrelationship between the child and parents and siblings; (4) any history of
domestic violence; (5) preference of
child; if of suitable age; (6) needs of
child; (7) stability of home environment
offered; (8) quality and continuity of
education; (9) fitness of parents;

(continued)

Custody (cont.)

(10) geographical proximity of the parties' homes; (11) extent and quality of time with the child before and after separation; (12) employment responsibilities; and (13) age and number of children. Judge must follow the parties agreement, unless he determines it is not in the child's best interest. Where parties don't agree, judge may require each party to submit a proposed custody plan.

Child Support

(1) needs of child; (2) standard of living and economic circumstances; (3) income and assets of parties; (4) earning ability of the parties; (5) child's need and capacity for education, including higher education; (6) age and health of parties and child; (7) income, assets and earning capacity of child; (8) other child support obligations of parties; (9) debts and liabilities of parties and child; and (10) any other relevant factor.
Termination age: 18.

Termination of
Parental Rights

Grounds: (1) child's health and development has been endangered by the parental relationship; (2) parent can't or won't provide a safe and stable home for the child; (3) termination of parental rights won't do more harm than good; and (4) abandonment.

New Mexico

The Law

New Mexico Statutes 1978 Annotated. **Example**: New Mexico Statutes Annotated, Chapter 40, Section 40-4-1 (N.M.S.A. Sec. 40-4-1).

Case Style

_____ JUDICIAL DISTRICT COURT COUNTY OF _____ STATE OF NEW MEXICO

Designation of Parties

_____, Petitioner vs. _____ Respondent

Custody

Best interest of the child considering: (1) wishes of parties; (2) wishes of child; (3) interaction and interrelationship between the child and parties, siblings and other significant persons; (4) child's adjustment to home, school and community; and (5) mental and physical condition of all persons involved.

(continued)

Custody

Joint custody is presumed in the child's best interest considering: (1) whether child has established a close relationship with each party; (2) whether each party is capable of providing care; (3) whether each party is willing to accept responsibilities of child care; (4) whether child can best maintain and strengthen a relationship with both parties and profit from such involvement; (5) whether each party is able to allow the other to provide care without intrusion; (6) the suitability of the parenting plan; (7) geographical distance between the parties' residences; and (8) the parties' willingness and ability to communicate and cooperate regarding the child's needs.

Child Support

State child support guidelines available from court clerk.
Termination age: 18.

Termination of Parental Rights

Grounds: (1) abandonment; (2) neglect or abuse of the child; and (3) child placed in the permanent care of others.

New York

The Law

McKinney's Consolidated Laws of New York Annotated. **Example**: Consolidated Laws of New York, Domestic Relations Law, Section 170 (C.L.N.Y., D.R.L. Sec. 170). These volumes are first divided into subjects, so be sure you find the correctly titled volumes, such as "Domestic Relations," "Estates, Powers and Trusts," "Probate," etc.

Case Style

SUPREME COURT OF THE STATE OF NEW YORK _____ COUNTY

Designation of Parties

_____, Plaintiff vs.
_____, Defendant

Custody

Best interest of the child.

Child Support

Based on a pro-rate share of the child's needs, according to the relative income of the parties. Needs are determined as a percentage of the parties' combined income as follows: 17% for one child; 25% for two children; 29% for three children; 31% for four children; and 35% or more for five or more children. This amount may be increased if certain special circumstances exist as stated in the state statute. Termination age: 18.

Termination of Parental Rights

Grounds: (1) abandonment; (2) parent surrender the child to an authorized agency; and (3) mental illness or mental retardation which renders parent incapable of taking care of the child.

North Carolina

The Law

General Statutes of North Carolina. **Example**: General Statutes of North Carolina, Chapter 50, Section 1 (G.S.N.C. Sec. 50-1). (Lawyers and judges commonly refer to these as the "North Carolina General Statutes," although that is not the title that appears on the covers of the volumes.)

Case Style

IN THE GENERAL COURT OF JUSTICE, _____ DIVISION, DISTRICT COURT NORTH CAROLINA, _____ COUNTY

Designation of Parties

_____ Plaintiff vs.
_____ Defendant

Custody

Best interest of the child.

Child Support

State child support guidelines available from court clerk.
Termination age: 18.

Termination of Parental Rights

Grounds: (1) parent has neglected or abused the child; (2) parent has willfully left child in foster care for more than 12 months; (3) parent is incapable of providing proper care and supervision for the child; and (4) abandonment.

North Dakota

<table>
<tr><td>The Law</td><td>North Dakota Century Code Annotated. Example: North Dakota Century Code, Title 14, Chapter 14-05, Section 14-05-01 (N.D.C.C. Sec. 14-05-01).</td></tr>
<tr><td>Case Style</td><td>STATE OF NORTH DAKOTA, COUNTY OF _____ IN THE DISTRICT COURT, _____ JUDICIAL DISTRICT</td></tr>
<tr><td>Designation of Parties</td><td>_____ Plaintiff vs.
_____ Defendant</td></tr>
<tr><td>Custody</td><td>(1) love, affection and emotional ties between child and each party; (2) each party's capacity and disposition to give love, affection and guidance and to continue the child's education; (3) each party's disposition to provide food, clothing, medical care and other material needs; (4) length of time the child has been in a stable, satisfactory environment and the desirability of maintaining continuity; (5) the permanence, as a family unit, of the existing or proposed custodial home; (6) moral fitness of the parties;</td></tr>
</table>

(continued)

Custody (cont.)	(7) mental and physical health of the parties; (8) child's home, school and community record; (9) the reasonable preference of the child, if of sufficient intelligence, understanding and experience; (10) an existence of domestic violence; (11) the interaction and interrelationship between the child and parties, siblings and other significant persons; and, (12) any other relevant factor.
Child Support	State child support guidelines available from court clerk. Termination age: 18.
Termination of Parental Rights	Grounds: (1) neglect by reason of misconduct, faults or habits of parent; (2) by reason of physical or mental incapacity the parent is unable to care for the child; and (3) child suffers from mental, moral or emotional harm.

Ohio

The Law

Page's Ohio Revised Code Annotated. **Example**: Ohio Revised Code, Title 31, Section 3105.01 (O.R.C. Sec. 3105.01).

Case Style

IN THE COURT OF COMMON PLEAS OF _____ COUNTY, OHIO

Designation
of Parties

_____ Plaintiff vs.
_____ Defendant

Custody

Best interest of the child, considering: (1) wishes of the parties; (2) child's wishes, if interviewed by judge; (3) the interaction and interrelationship between the child and parties, siblings and other significant persons; (4) child's adjustment to home, school and community; (5) mental and physical condition of all persons involved; (6) party more likely to honor and facilitate visitation; (7) compliance with any child support orders; (8) any history of abuse or neglect; (9) any history of visitation denial; and (10) whether a party intends to make his or her residence outside of Ohio.

(continued)

Child Support

(1) child's resources and earning ability; (2) parties' resources and assets; (3) physical and emotional condition and needs of child; (4) child's need and capacity for education; (5) child's age; (6) parties' other support obligations; and (7) value of services contributed by custodial parent. Child support order must provide for medical insurance payment through the child support enforcement agency and one of the income withholding orders or cash bonds.

Termination age: 18.

*Termination of
Parental Rights*

Grounds: (1) abandonment; and (2) abuse and neglect.

Oklahoma

The Law	Oklahoma Statutes Annotated. ***Example***: Oklahoma Statutes Annotated, Title 43, Section 101 (43 O.S.A. Sec. 101).
Case Style	STATE OF OKLAHOMA, IN THE DISTRICT COURT,_____ COUNTY
Designation of Parties	_____ Plaintiff vs. _____ Defendant
Custody	(1) physical, mental and moral welfare of the child; and (2) child's preference. If domestic violence is involved it is presumed that it is against the best interest of the child for the guilty party to have custody.
Child Support	Factors: (1) income and means of the parties; and (2) the property and assets of the parties. Termination age: 18.
Termination of Parental Rights	Grounds: (1) abandonment; (2) child has been adjudicated to be deprived; (3) best interest of the child; (4) parent convicted of criminal act relating to child abuse or neglect; (5) physical or sexual abuse of child by parent; and (6) parent has a mental illness or deficiency which renders him or her incapable of caring for the child.

Oregon

The Law	Oregon Revised Statutes Annotated. ***Example***: Oregon Revised Statutes, Chapter 107, Section 107.015 (O.R.S. Sec. 107.015).
Case Style	IN THE CIRCUIT COURT THE STATE OF OREGON THE COUNTY OF
Designation of Parties	_____ Petitioner vs. _____ Respondent
Custody	Joint custody only awarded where both parties agree. Factors: (1) emotional ties between the child and other family members; (2) each party's interest in and attitude toward the child; (3) desirability of continuing existing relationships; and (4) any abuse of one party by the other. Conduct and life-style are only considered if it is causing or may cause emotional of physical damage to the child (this is usually very difficult to prove).

(continued)

Child Support

Factors: (1) evidence of the other available resources of a parent; (2) the reasonable necessities of a parent; (3) the net income; (4) parent's ability to borrow; (5) number and needs of other dependents of a parent; (6) medical circumstances of a parent; (7) needs of the child; (8) desirability of the custodial parent remaining in the home as a full-time parent and homemaker; and, (9) tax consequences. Termination age: 18.

Termination of Parental Rights

Grounds: (1) physical and sexual abuse of the child by the parent; (2) abuse or neglect of any child resulting in death; (3) emotional illness, mental illness or mental deficiency which renders parent incapable of caring for child; (4) addictive or habitual use of alcohol or drugs; and, (5) neglect of child.

Pennsylvania

The Law

Purdon's Pennsylvania Consolidated Statutes Annotated. ***Example***: Pennsylvania Consolidated Statutes Annotated, Title 23, Section 3101 (23 Pa.C.S.A. Sec. 3101).

Case Style

COURT OF COMMON PLEAS, _____ COUNTY, PENNSYLVANIA

Designation
of Parties

_____ Plaintiff vs.
_____ Defendant

Custody

Best interest of the child based upon which parent is more likely to encourage and allow frequent and continuing contact with the other parent. If joint custody is desired, court may require written custody plan.

Child Support

State child support award based on reasonable needs of the child and ability of parent to provide support. Primary emphasis is placed on net incomes and earning capacities of the parents. Termination age: 21.

Termination of
Parental Rights

Grounds: (1) abuse and/or neglect; (2) child removed from parents by the court; and (3) child conceived as a result of rape or incest; and abandonment.

Rhode Island

The Law	General Laws of Rhode Island. ***Example***: General Laws of Rhode Island, Section 15-5-1 (G.L.R.I. Sec. 15-5-1). Ignore "Title" and "Chapter" numbers.
Case Style	STATE OF RHODE ISLAND, FAMILY COURT _____ DIVISION [Check with court clerk for division designation]
Designation of Parties	_____ Plaintiff vs. _____ Defendant
Custody	Best interest of the child.
Child Support	Factors: (1) financial resources of the child; (2) financial resources of the custodial parent (3) physical and emotional condition of the child and his or her educational needs; and (4) financial resources and needs of the non-custodial parent. Termination age: 18.
Termination of Parental Rights	Grounds: (1) parent willfully neglected to provide care and maintenance for child; (2) parent is unfit by reason of conduct or conditions detrimental to the child; (3) emotional illness, mental illness, mental deficiency of the parent; (4) conduct toward any child of a cruel or abusive nature; (5) child has been placed in custody or care of department for children; and (6) abandonment.

South Carolina

The Law	Code of Laws of South Carolina. ***Example***: Code of Laws of South Carolina, Title 20, Section 20-3-10 (C.L.S.C. Sec. 20-3-10).
Case Style	STATE OF SOUTH CAROLINA, THE _____ COURT OF THE _____ JUDICIAL DISTRICT
Designation of Parties	_____ Plaintiff vs. _____ Defendant
Custody	Determined "... as from the circumstances of the parties and the nature of the case and the best spiritual as well as other interests of the children as may be fit, equitable and just."
Child Support	Same factors as for custody, and "... a fair and reasonable sum according to his or her means,as may be determined by the court." Termination age: 18.
Termination of Parental Rights	Grounds: (1) best interest of the child; (2) child or another child in home harmed as a result of abuse or neglect; (3) abandonment; (4) alcohol and drug addiction; and (5) parent is mentally deficient or ill and cannot take care of child.

South Dakota

The Law	South Dakota Codified Laws. ***Example***: South Dakota Codified Laws, Title 25, Chapter 25-4, Section 25-4-1 (S.D.C.L. Sec. 25-4-1).
Case Style	STATE OF SOUTH DAKOTA, COUNTY OF _____, IN THE CIRCUIT COURT, _____ JUDICIAL DISTRICT
Designation of Parties	_____ Plaintiff vs. _____ Defendant
Custody	Only factor referenced in state statute is that custody is to be determined "as may seem necessary and proper."
Child Support	State child support guidelines available at S.D.C.L. Sec. 25-7-6.2. Termination age: 18.
Termination of Parental Rights	Abandonment is the only statutory factor.

Tennessee

The Law

Tennessee Code Annotated. *Example*: Tennessee Code Annotated, Title 36, Section 36-4-101 (T.C.A. Sec. 36-4-101).

Case Style

IN THE _____ COURT OF _____ COUNTY, TENNESSEE

Designation of Parties

_____ Petitioner vs.
_____ Respondent

Custody

Best interests of the child considering the following factors: (1) love, affection and emotional ties between parents and child; (2) disposition of parents to provide food, clothing, medical care, education and other necessary care and degree to which parent has become the primary caregiver; (3) importance of continuity in the child's life and length of time child has lived in a stable, satisfactory environment; (4) stability of the family unit; (5) mental and physical health of parents; (6) child's home, school and community record; (7) reasonable preference of child at least 12 years of age; (8) any evidence of physical or emotional abuse of child, parent or others; and (9) character and behavior of any person who resides in or frequents the home and that person's interaction with the child.

(continued)

Child Support

State child support guidelines available from court clerk. Termination age: 18.

Termination of Parental Rights

Grounds: (1) best interest of the child; (2) abandonment; (3) child removed from home of parent by order of court; (4) parent committed severe child abuse; (5) parent incarcerated for conduct against the child; (6) parent sentenced to a term of 10 or more years in prison; and (7) parent incompetent to care for child.

Texas

The Law	Vernon's Texas Code Annotated. ***Example***: Texas Code Annotated, Family Code, Chapter 3, Section 3.01 (T.C.A., F.C. Sec. 3.01).
Case Style	IN THE DISTRICT COURT OF ____ COUNTY, TEXAS, JUDICIAL DISTRICT ____
Designation of Parties	_____ Petitioner vs. _____ Respondent

Custody

Called "managing conservatorship." Factors include: (1) qualifications of the parent; and (2) any evidence of intentional use of abusive force against spouse or any person under age 18 within the past two years. Joint custody may be granted after the judge considers: (1) if joint custody will benefit child's physical, psychological and emotional needs and development; (2) ability of parties to give child first priority and reach shared decisions; (3) ability to encourage relationship between the child and other parent; (4) whether both parents participated in rearing the child before filing; (5) geographical proximity of the parent's homes; (6) preferences of the child if at least 12; and (7) any other relevant factor.

(continued)

Child Support   If payor's monthly net resources are under $6000, then a percentage of monthly net resources as follows: 20% for one child, 25% for two children, 30% for three children, 35% for four children, 40% for five children, and over 40% for six or more children. If net resources are over $600, then may order additional child support. Termination age: 18.

Termination of   Grounds: (1) danger to physical health or
Parental Rights   safety by parent; (2) abuse or neglect; and (3) sexual abuse of another child by the parent.

Utah

The Law	Utah Code Annotated 1953. **Example**: Utah Code, Title 30, Chapter 3, Section 30-3-1 (U.C. Sec. 30-3-1).
Case Style	IN THE DISTRICT COURT OF THE _____ JUDICIAL DISTRICT, IN AND FOR _____, COUNTY, STATE OF UTAH
Designation of Parties	_____ Plaintiff vs. _____ Defendant
Custody	Best interest of the child considering: (1) past conduct and demonstrated moral standards of the parties; (2) child's wishes; (3) which party is most likely to act in the child's best interest, including allowing contact with the other party; and (4) any other relevant factor.
Child Support	State child support guidelines available at U.C. Sec. 78-45-7. Termination age: 18.
Termination of Parental Rights	Grounds: (1) abandonment; (2) neglect or abuse; and (3) parent unfit or incompetent.

Vermont

The Law	Vermont Statutes Annotated. ***Example***: Vermont Statutes Annotated, Title 15, Section 551 (15 V.S.A. Sec. 551). Ignore "chapter" numbers.

Case Style

STATE OF VERMONT, SUPERIOR COURT, _____ COUNTY

Designation
of Parties

_____ Plaintiff vs.

_____ Defendant

Custody

Best interest of the child considering: (1) relationship of the child and each party, and each party's ability and disposition to provide love, affection and guidance; (2) ability and disposition to provide food, clothing, medical care, other material needs, and a safe environment; (3) ability and disposition to meet the child's present and future developmental needs; (4) quality of the child's adjustment to present housing, school and community, and potential effect of a change; (5) ability and disposition to foster a continuing relationship with the other party; (6) quality of the child's relationship with primary caregiver; (7) child's relationship to other significant persons; (8) ability and disposition of the parties to make joint decisions; and (9) any evidence of abuse.

(continued)

Child Support	State child support guidelines available from court clerk. Termination age: 18.
Termination of Parental Rights	Grounds: (1) parent doesn't exercise parental responsibility for the child; (2) fails to support the child in accordance with financial means; (3) parent convicted of a crime of violence; and (4) risk of substantial harm to physical or psychological well-being of child.

Virginia

The Law	Code of Virginia 1950. ***Example***: Code of Virginia, Title 20, Section 20-91 (C.V. Sec. 20-91). Ignore "chapter" numbers; look for "title" and "section" numbers.
Case Style	VIRGINIA: IN THE _____ COURT OF _____ [Call the clerk or look in a court file to see what should go in the blanks]
Designation of Parties	_____ Plaintiff vs. _____ Defendant
Custody	Best interest of the child considering: (1) age, physical and mental condition of the child and the parties; (2) relationship between the child and each party; (3) needs of child; (4) the role each party played and will play in the child's upbringing and care; (5) any history of family abuse; (6) propensity of each parent to support a relationship and contact with the child and the other parent; (7) child's preference if suitable age, intelligence and understanding; and (8) any other relevant factor.
Child Support	State child support guidelines can be found at C.V. Sec. 20-108.2. Termination age: 18.

(continued)

Termination of
Parental Rights

Grounds: (1) mental and emotional illness or mental defect of parent; (2) habitual substance abuse by parent; and (3) neglect or abuse of the child by the parent.

Washington

The Law	West's Revised Code of Washington Annotated. ***Example***: Revised Code of Washington Annotated, Title 26, Chapter 26.09, Section 26.09.010 (R.C.W.A. Sec. 26.09.010).

Case Style

IN THE _____ COURT OF THE STATE OF WASHINGTON, IN AND FOR THE COUNTY OF

_____

[depending upon the term used in your county, either the word "SUPERIOR" or "FAMILY" goes in the first blank]

Designation of Parties

_____ Petitioner vs.

_____ Respondent

Custody

Factors: (1) each party's relative strength, nature and stability of the relationship with the child including which party has taken greater responsibility for the child; (2) any agreement between the parties; (3) each party's past and potential for future performance of parenting functions; (4) child's emotional needs and development; (5) the child's relationship with siblings and other significant adults and involvement in his or her physical surroundings, school and other activities; (6) the wishes of the parties and the child; and (7) each party's employment schedule. The greatest weight is given to factor (1) above.

(continued)

Child Support

State child support guidelines can be found in Title 26, Chapter 26.19 of the Revised Code. Termination age: 18.

Termination of
Parental Rights

Grounds: (1) habitual substance abuse by parent; and (2) psychological incapacity or mental deficiency of parent.

West Virginia

The Law

West Virginia Code. **Example**: West Virginia Code, Chapter 48, Article 2, Section 48-2-1 (W.V.C. Sec. 48-2-1).

Case Style

CIRCUIT COURT OF _____ COUNTY, WEST VIRGINIA

Designation
of Parties

_____ Plaintiff vs.
_____ Defendant

Custody

No statutory factors. Presumption in favor of primary caretaker.

Child Support

Child support determined by dividing the total child support obligation between the parents in proportion to their income using their adjusted gross income. Termination age: 18.

Termination of
Parental Rights

Grounds: (1) abandonment; and (2) abuse or neglect.

Wisconsin

The Law	West's Wisconsin Statutes Annotated. **Example**: Wisconsin Statutes Annotated, Section 767.001 (W.S.A. Sec. 767.001). Ignore "chapter" numbers.

Case Style

STATE OF WISCONSIN: CIRCUIT COURT, _____ COUNTY

Designation of Parties

_____ Petitioner vs.

_____ Respondent

Custody

Referred to as "legal custody and physical placement." Best interest of the child considering: (1) wishes of parties; (2) wishes of child; (3) interaction and inter-relationship between child and the parties, siblings and any other significant person; (4) child's adjustment to home, school and community; (5) mental and physical health of all parties involved; (6) availability of public and private child care services; (7) whether one is likely to unreasonably interfere with child's continuing relationship with the other party; (8) any evidence of child abuse; (9) any evidence of domestic abuse; (9) whether either party has had a significant problem with alcohol or drug abuse; and (11) any other relevant factor.

(continued)

Child Support	Child support determined by formula, with 17% of gross income awarded for one child, 25% for two children, 29% for three children, 34% for five or more children. This may be reduced according to the amount of time the payor spends with the child. Termination age: 18.
Termination of Parental Rights	Grounds: (1) abandonment; (2) continuing need of protection or services; (3) continuing parental responsibility; (4) child abuse; (5) failure to assume parental responsibility; (6) incestuous parenthood; and (7) intentional killing of opposing parent.

Wyoming

The Law	Wyoming Statutes Annotated. ***Example***: Wyoming Statutes Annotated, Title 20, Chapter 2, Section 20-2-104 (W.S.A. Sec. 20-2-104).
Case Style	IN THE DISTRICT COURT IN AND FOR _____ COUNTY, WYOMING
Designation of Parties	_____ Plaintiff vs. _____ Defendant
Custody	Custody to be determined "... as appears most expedient and beneficial for the well-being of the children. The court shall consider the relative competency of both parents and no award of custody shall be made solely on the basis of gender of parent."
Child Support	Factors: (1) age of child; (2) cost of necessary child day care; (3) special health care and educational needs of the child; (4) expenses reasonable related to the mother's pregnancy if the parents were never married; (5) cost of transportation of the child to and from visitation; and (6) amount of time the child spends with each parent. Termination age: 18.
Termination of Parental Rights	Grounds: (1) abandonment; (2) neglect or abuse; and (3) parental incarceration and unfitness.

APPENDIX B:
SAMPLE FORMS

This appendix contains sample forms which are typical of those used in most states. However, because each state is different (and sometimes each county is different), you will need to do some research to be sure your forms will be accepted by the courts in your state and county. Before following the forms in this appendix, be sure you:

- read the information for your state in appendix A of this book;
- check with your clerk of court to find out if there are any official forms you can or must use. If so, use the official forms; and,
- review one or more court files of the type of case you will be filing at your court clerk's office to see how papers are prepared in your area, then use the same format.

The sample forms in this appendix have been completed based upon the following information for a fictional state.

SUPERIOR

The Law:	Superior Statutes Annotated. ***Example:*** Superior Statutes Annotated, Title 40, Chapter 1, Section 40-1-101 (S.S.A. Sec. 40-1-101).
Case Style:	IN THE _____ CIRCUIT COURT, IN AND FOR _____ COUNTY, SUPERIOR
Designation of Parties:	_____, Plaintiff, and _____, Defendant.

Custody:	Best interest of the child, considering: (1) age and sex of child; (2) wishes of parents and child; (3) interaction and interrelationship between the child and parents, siblings, and other significant persons; and (4) mental and physical health of all persons involved.
Child Support:	Child support guidelines found in S.S. A. §40-4-130. Termination age: 18.
Termination of Parental Rights:	Grounds: (1) abandonment; (2) emotional or mental illness or mental deficiency of parent; (3) excessive substance abuse by parent; (4) child abused or neglected, or in danger of abuse, by parent; or (5) parent convicted and imprisoned for felony.

TABLE OF FORMS

```
IN THE FIFTH CIRCUIT COURT, IN AND FOR
     COLUMBIA COUNTY, SUPERIOR
```

Jane Doe,
> Plaintiff,

vs.   CASE NO: _____

John Smith,
> Defendant.

COMPLAINT FOR PATERNITY
Plaintiff alleges the following:

1. This is an action seeking the establishment of paternity pursuant to __S.S.A., Section 42-2-101_____.

2. The Plaintiff is a citizen and resident of _Columbia County Superior_____. Based upon information and belief, Plaintiff alleges that the Defendant is a citizen and resident of __Columbia County, Superior_____.

3. The minor child named __Veronica Doe_____, was born on _February 14, 2003__, in __Columbia_____ County, __Superior_____.

4. The Plaintiff is the minor child's biological mother.

5. The Plaintiff believes that the Defendant is the minor child's biological father based upon the following facts and circumstances:

☒   a.   At the time of both conception and delivery of the minor child, the Plaintiff was not married to the Defendant nor married to anyone else.

☒   b.   The Plaintiff and Defendant had sexual relations during the months preceding the birth of the child.

216

☒   c.   Other: The Plaintiff has blood type A,
the minor child has blood type O, and
the Defendant has informed the
Plaintiff that he has blood type O.

6. There are no custody or visitation actions with respect to the minor child which are currently pending.

7. Inasmuch as a question as to the parentage of the minor child has arisen in this action, Plaintiff moves the Court for entry of an order directing that Plaintiff, Defendant, and the minor child submit to genetic testing, HLA blood testing and/or other appropriate blood tests and comparisons which have been developed and adapted for purposes of establishing or disproving parentage and which are reasonably accessible to the parties involved.

Wherefore, Plaintiff prays the Court as follows:

1. That the Court enter an Order directing that Plaintiff and Defendant and the minor child named above submit to genetic testing, HLA blood testing and/or any other tests and comparison which have been developed and adapted for the purposes of establishing or   disproving parentage and which are reasonably assessable to the parties involved.

2. That this verified complaint be taken as an affidavit upon which upon which the Court can base all of its orders in this case.

3. That the costs of this action be taxed to the ~~Plaintiff~~/Defendant.

4. That the Court grant to Plaintiff such other and further relief as may be just and proper.

This 16th day of _____ March _____, 2003 .

_____ *Jane Doe* _____

Pro Se

Name: Jane Doe
Address: 127 Walnut Street
            Superior City, SU 99999
Telephone: (222) 555-5155

IN THE FIFTH CIRCUIT COURT, IN AND FOR
COLUMBIA COUNTY, SUPERIOR

Jane Doe,
       Plaintiff,

vs.   CASE NO: _____

John Smith,
       Defendant.

COMPLAINT FOR CUSTODY

Plaintiff / Petitioner alleges the following:

1. This is an action seeking temporary and permanent custody of a minor child(ren), pursuant to _S.S.A., Section 42-3-105_.

2. The Plaintiff / Petitioner is a citizen and resident of _Columbia County, Superior_. Based upon information and belief, Plaintiff / Petitioner alleges that the Defendant / Respondent is a citizen and resident of _Columbia County, Superior_ _____.

3. The Plaintiff / Petitioner is the ____mother____ of the minor child(ren): ___Veronica Doe___, born ___February 14, 2003_____ _____ respectively.

4. The Defendant / Respondent is the minor child(ren)'s ___father___.

5. Plaintiff / Petitioner is a fit and proper person to have the general care, custody, and control of the minor child(ren).

6. It is in the best interest of the minor child(ren) that custody be awarded to the Plaintiff / Petitioner.

WHEREFORE, Plaintiff / ~~Petitioner~~ prays the court for relief as follows:

1. That the foregoing Complaint / ~~Petition~~ be accepted as an affidavit in support of the Plaintiff's / ~~Petitioner's~~ application for both temporary and permanent custody of the minor child(~~ren~~), and that said Complaint /x~~Petition~~ also be allowed and taken as an affidavit upon which to base all orders of the Court.

2. That an order be entered herein awarding the temporary and permanent custody of the minor child(~~ren~~) to the Plaintiff / ~~Petitioner~~

3. That the Court grant such other and further relief as it deems just and proper.

This ___16th___ day of _____March_____, ___2003__.

_____*Jane Doe*_____

Pro Se

Name:___Jane Doe_____

Address: __127 Walnut Street_____

_____Superior City, SU 99999____

Telephone: _(222) 555-5155_____

IN THE FIFTH CIRCUIT COURT, IN AND FOR
COLUMBIA COUNTY, SUPERIOR

John Smith,
       Petitioner,

vs.   CASE NO: _____

Jane Doe,
       Respondent.

PETITION FOR VISITATION

~~Plaintiff~~/ Petitioner alleges the following:

1. This is an action seeking visitation with a minor child(ren), pursuant to __S.S.A., Section 42-3-105__.

2. The ~~Plaintiff~~ / Petitioner is a citizen and resident of __Columbia County, Superior__. Based upon information and belief, ~~Plaintiff~~/ Petitioner alleges that the ~~Defendant~~ / Respondent is a citizen and resident of __Columbia County, Superior__
_____.

3. The ~~Plaintiff~~/ Petitioner is the __father__ of the minor child(~~ren~~): __Veronica Doe__
_____,
born __February 14, 2003__
_____ ~~respectively~~.

4. The ~~Defendant~~ / Respondent is the minor child(~~ren~~)'s __mother__.

5. ~~Plaintiff~~/ Petitioner is a fit and proper person to have visitation privileges with the minor child(~~ren~~).

6. It is in the best interest of the minor child(~~ren~~) that visitation privileges be awarded to the ~~Plaintiff~~/ Petitioner.

220

WHEREFORE, ~~Plaintiff~~/ Petitioner prays the court for relief as
follows:

1. That the foregoing ~~Complaint~~ / Petition be accepted as an
affidavit in support of the ~~Plaintiff's~~ / Petitioner's application for visitation with the minor child(~~ren~~), and that said ~~Complaint~~ / Petition
also be allowed and taken as an affidavit upon which to base all
orders of the Court.

2. That an order be entered awarding the following visitation
privileges to the ~~Plaintiff~~ Petitioner.

```
Alternate weekends from 7:00 p.m. Friday until
4:00 p.m. Sunday; alternating holidays of New
Years Day, Easter,Memorial Day, Fourth of July,
Labor Day, Thanksgiving Day, Christmas Eve, and
Christmas Day; every Father's Day; and one week
during summer vacation from school.
```

3. That the Court grant such other and further relief as it deems
just and proper.

This <u>16th</u> day of <u>March</u>, <u>2003</u>.

John Smith

Pro Se

Name: John Smith

Address: 1482 Lakeshore Drive
Superior City, SU 99999

Telephone: (222) 555-5555

IN THE FIFTH CIRCUIT COURT, IN AND FOR
COLUMBIA COUNTY, SUPERIOR

Jane Doe,
    Plaintiff,

vs.   CASE NO: _____

John Smith,
    Defendant.

CHILD SUPPORT COMPLAINT

Plaintiff / P̶e̶t̶i̶t̶i̶o̶n̶e̶r̶ alleges the following:

1. This is an action seeking child support on behalf of a minor child(ren), pursuant to S.S.A., Section 42-3-106 .

2. The Plaintiff / P̶e̶t̶i̶t̶i̶o̶n̶e̶r̶ is a citizen and resident of Columbia County, SU . Based upon information and belief, Plaintiff / P̶e̶t̶i̶t̶i̶o̶n̶e̶r̶ alleges that the Defendant / R̶e̶s̶p̶o̶n̶d̶e̶n̶t̶ is a citizen and resident of Columbia County, SU .

3. The Plaintiff / P̶e̶t̶i̶t̶i̶o̶n̶e̶r̶ is the mother of the minor child(r̶e̶n̶): Veronica Doe _____,
born February 14, 2003 _____ r̶e̶s̶p̶e̶c̶t̶i̶v̶e̶l̶y̶.

4. The Defendant / R̶e̶s̶p̶o̶n̶d̶e̶n̶t̶ is the minor child(r̶e̶n̶)'s father .

5. The minor child(r̶e̶n̶) has/have been in the actual physical custody of the Plaintiff / P̶e̶t̶i̶t̶i̶o̶n̶e̶r̶ since February 14, 2003 .

6. The Defendant / R̶e̶s̶p̶o̶n̶d̶e̶n̶t̶ is able-bodied and capable of providing financial support on behalf of the minor child(r̶e̶n̶). He/s̶h̶e̶ is employed at Superior Auto Repair and earns approximately $ 26,000.00 per year.

7. The minor child(r̶e̶n̶) is in need of support.

8. The minor child(r̶e̶n̶) ___has/have X has no/h̶a̶v̶e̶ ̶n̶o̶ extraordinary expenses.

WHEREFORE, Plaintiff / ~~Petitioner~~ prays the court for relief as follows:

1. That the foregoing Complaint / ~~Petition~~ be accepted as an affidavit in support of the Plaintiff's / ~~Petitioner's~~ application for child support and that this ~~Complaint~~ / Petition also be allowed and taken as an affidavit upon which to base all orders of the Court.

2. That an order be entered directing the Defendant / ~~Respondent~~ to pay child support pursuant to the child support guidelines.

3. That the Court grant such other and further relief as it deems just and proper.

This __16th__ day of _____March_____, ____2003__.

Jane Doe
_____
                                        Pro Se
Name:__Jane Doe_____
Address: _127 Walnut Street_____
_____Superior City, SU 99999___
Telephone: _(222) 555-5155_____

IN THE FIFTH CIRCUIT COURT, IN AND FOR
COLUMBIA COUNTY, SUPERIOR

Jane Doe,
      Petitioner,

vs.   CASE NO: _____

John Smith,
      Respondent.

PETITION TO TERMINATE PARENTAL RIGHTS

The Petitioner alleges the following:

1. This is an action seeking the termination of the parental rights of the Respondent pursuant to <u>S.S.A., Section 102-1-201</u>
_____.

2. The name(s) of the minor child(ren) who is/are the subject of this petition is/are: <u>Veronica Doe</u>
_____,
born <u>February 14, 2003</u>
_____ respectively.

3. The Respondent is the biological father of the minor child(ren) and is believed to reside in <u>Columbia County, Superior</u>
_____.

4. The Petitioner is the biological mother of the minor child(ren); and resides in <u>Columbia County, Superior</u>
_____ and has so resided there with the minor child(ren) since _____
<u>February 16,</u>_____, <u>2003</u>.

5. The Petitioner and the Respondent were never married and the Petitioner has had the actual physical custody of the minor child(ren) since _____<u>February 14,</u>_____, <u>1999</u>.

6. ☒   No person has been appointed as guardian ad litem for the minor child(~~ren~~) in this or any other action.

    ❏   _____

has been appointed as guardian ad litem for the minor child(ren) in this action.

7. The parental rights of the Respondent are subject to termination because:

The Respondent has abandoned the minor child, by failing to provide any financial support and failing to make any attempt to contact the minor child since the child's birth.

_____

_____

8. This petition has not been filed to circumvent any provisions of the Uniform Child Custody Jurisdiction Act.

WHEREFORE, the Petitioner prays that the parental rights of the Respondent be terminated.

This __16th__ day of _____March_____, ___2003___.

          _____*Jane Doe*_____

                                   Pro Se

Name: __Jane Doe_____

Address: __127 Walnut Street_____

            __Superior City, SU 99999_____

Telephone: __(222) 555-5155_____

VERIFICATION

I, _____Jane Doe_____ being first duly sworn, depose and say:

That I am the Plaintiff in this action;

That I have read the foregoing ___ Complaint _X_ Petition ___ Motion and know the contents thereof;

That the same is true of my own knowledge, save and except those matters and things therein stated upon information and belief, and as to those matters and things, I believe them to be true.

This _16th_ day of _____March_____, ___2003__ .

_____*Jane Doe*_____
                                                                    Affiant

STATE OF _____
COUNTY OF _____
Sworn to and subscribed before me this _____ day of _____, _____.

_____
Notary Public
My Commission Expires: _____

IN THE FIFTH CIRCUIT COURT, IN AND FOR
COLUMBIA COUNTY, SUPERIOR

Jane Doe,
     Plaintiff,

vs.   CASE NO: _____

John Smith,
     Defendant.

Uniform Child Custody Jurisdiction Act Affidavit

1. The name and present address of each child (under 18) in this case is:

     Veronica Doe
     127 Walnut Street
     Superior City, SU 99999

2. The places where the child(ren) has/have lived within the last 5 years are:

     127 Walnut Street
     Superior City, SU 99999

3. The name(s) and present address(es) of custodians with whom the child(ren) has/have lived within the past 5 years are:

     Jane Doe
     127 Walnut Street
     Superior City, SU 99999

4. I do not know of and have not participated (as a party, witness, or in any other capacity) in any other court decision, order, or proceeding (including divorce, separate maintenance, child neglect, dependency, or guardianship) concerning the custody or visitation of the child(ren) in this state or any other state, except: [Specify case name and number and court's name and address.]

     none

5. I do not have information of any proceeding (including divorce, separate maintenance, child neglect, dependency or guardianship) concerning the custody or visitation of the child(ren), in this state or any other state except: [specify case name and number and court's name and address.]

    none

That proceeding ___ is continuing ___ has been stayed by the court.

___ Temporary action by this court is necessary to protect the child(ren) because the child(ren) has/have been subjected to or threatened with mistreatment or abut or is/are otherwise neglected or dependent.

[Attach explanation.]

6. I do not know of any person who is not already a party to this proceeding who has physical custody of, or who claims to have custody or visitation rights with, the child(ren), except: [state name(s) and address(es).]

    none

7. The child(ren)'s "home state" is ___Superior___
["Home State" means the state in which the child(ren) immediately preceding the time involved lived with his or her parents, a parent, or a person acting as a parent, for at least 6 consecutive months, and, in the case of a child less than 6 months old, the state in which the child lived from birth with any of the persons mentioned. Periods of temporary absence of the named persons are counted as a part of the 6 month or other period.]

I acknowledge a continuing duty to advise this court of any custody or visitation proceeding (including dissolution of marriage, separate maintenance, child neglect, or dependent) concerning the child(ren) in this state or any other state about which information is obtained during this proceeding.

This __16th__ day of _____March_____, __2003__.

_____*Jane Doe*_____

Signature of Affiant

Name_____Jane Doe_____

Address ___127 Walnut Street_____

_____Superior City, SU 99999_____

Telephone No. ___(222) 555-5155_____

STATE OF _____

COUNTY OF _____

Sworn to and subscribed before me this _____ day
of _____, _____.

_____

Notary Public
My Commission Expires: _____

IN THE FIFTH CIRCUIT COURT, IN AND FOR
COLUMBIA COUNTY, SUPERIOR

Jane Doe,
      Plaintiff,

vs.   CASE NO: <u>99-421</u>

John Smith,
      Defendant.

ANSWER

Defendant/~~Respondent~~ answering the allegations of the Plaintiff/~~Petitioner~~ alleges the following:

1. The allegations contained in paragraphs <u>1 through 3</u> _____ of the <u>Child Support Complaint</u> are true and correct.

2. The allegations contained in paragraphs <u>4 through 8</u> _____ are denied.

WHEREFORE, Defendant / ~~Respondent~~ prays the court for relief as follows:

1. That the foregoing Answer be allowed and taken as an affidavit upon which to base all orders of the Court.

2. That an order be entered _____ <u>dismissing the Child Support Complaint</u> _____.

3. That the Court grant such other and further relief as it deems just and proper.

This <u>29th</u> day of <u>March</u>, <u>2003</u>.

John Smith
_____
                                              Pro Se

Name <u>John Smith</u>
Address <u>1482 Lakeshore Dr.</u>
            <u>Superior City, SU 99999</u>
Telephone No. <u>222-555-5555</u>

230 *form i*

IN THE FIFTH CIRCUIT COURT, IN AND FOR
COLUMBIA COUNTY, SUPERIOR

Jane Doe,
         Plaintiff,

vs.   CASE NO: _____

John Smith,
         Defendant.

SUMMONS

TO: Each Sheriff of the State of __Superior_____.

YOU ARE COMMANDED to serve this Summons and a copy of
the Complaint / ~~Petition~~ in this action on the Defendant(s) /
~~Respondent(s)~~):

          John Smith
          1482 Lakeshore Drive
          Superior City, SU 99999

The Defendant(s) / ~~Respondent(s)~~ is /~~are~~ required to serve written
defenses to the Complaint / ~~Petition~~ on the Plaintiff(s) /
~~Petitioner(s)~~   Jane Doe
          127 Walnut Street
          Superior City, SU 99999

within __20___ calendar days after this Summons is served on the
Defendant(s) / ~~Respondent(s)~~, exclusive of the day of service, and
to file the original of the defenses with the clerk of this court either
before service on the Plaintiff(s) / ~~Petitioner(s)~~ or immediately
thereafter.

If any Defendant / Respondent fails to serve and file defenses as stated above, a default may be entered against the Defendant / Respondent for the relief demanded in the Complaint / Petition.

This __16th__ day of ___March_____, __2003____.

CLERK OF THE COURT

By:_____

IN THE FIFTH CIRCUIT COURT, IN AND FOR
COLUMBIA COUNTY, SUPERIOR

Jane Doe,
     Plaintiff,

vs.   CASE NO: __99-421__

John Smith,
     Defendant.

CERTIFICATE OF SERVICE

I, _____Jane Doe_____,
certify that a copy of the __Plaintiff's Financial Affidavit__
_____ was served upon the opposing
party or his/her attorney by depositing a copy of the same in
the United States mail with prepaid, first-class postage, and
addressed as follows: John Smith
                         1482 Lakeshore Dr.
                         Superior City, SU   99999
This _19th____ day of ____March_____, __2003____ .

Jane Doe
Name: ___Jane Doe_____
Address: __127 Walnut Street___
             Superior City, SU 99999
Telephone: _222-555-5155_____

IN THE FIFTH CIRCUIT COURT, IN AND FOR
COLUMBIA COUNTY, SUPERIOR

Jane Doe,
　　　Plaintiff,

vs.

CASE NO: __99-421__

John Smith,
　　　Defendant.

NOTICE OF HEARING

To:　John Smith

PLEASE TAKE NOTICE that the __Child Support Complaint__
will be called for hearing on _____Friday_____, the __23rd__
day of ____April____, __2003__, at __9:00__ _A_.M., before
the Honorable __Barry D. Hatchett__, Judge of
the above-titled court, at _Room 245, Columbia County Courth_ouse,
12 Main Street, Superior City, SU 99999.

_____*Jane Doe*_____
　　　　　　　　　　　　　　　　Signature
　　　Name: ____Jane Doe____
　　　Address: __127 Walnut Street__
　　　　　　__Superior City, SU 99999__
　　　Telephone: _222-555-5155_

IN THE FIFTH CIRCUIT COURT, IN AND FOR
COLUMBIA COUNTY, SUPERIOR

Jane Doe,
      Plaintiff,

vs.   CASE NO: __99-421_____

John Smith,
          Defendant.

SUBPOENA

TO: Payroll Clerk
      Superior Auto Repair
      42918 24th Street
      Superior, SU 99999

YOU ARE HEREBY COMMANDED to appear before the
Honorable Barry D. Hatchett _____,
Judge of the Court, at _Room 245, Columbia County_____
Courthouse, 12 Main Street, Superior City, SU 99999 ,
on ____Friday_____, ___April 23_____, _2003__, at
9:00_____ o'clock _A._. M., to:

[check all that apply]

☒   testify in the above-entitled action.

☒   produce the following items:

IF YOU FAIL TO APPEAR,
YOU MAY BE IN CONTEMPT OF COURT.

You are subpoenaed to appear by the attorney or party designated below, and unless excused from this subpoena by said attorney or party, or by the court, you shall respond to this subpoena as
directed.

If you have any questions about being subpoenaed as a witness, you should contact the attorney or party listed below who had the subpoena issued

This __12th__ day of _____April_____, __2003__ .

CLERK OF THE COURT

By:_____

Attorney or Party Requesting Subpoena:

Name:__Jane Doe_____
Address: __127 Walnut Street_____
____Superior City, SU 99999____
Telephone No.__222-555-5155_____

IN THE FIFTH CIRCUIT COURT, IN AND FOR
COLUMBIA COUNTY, SUPERIOR

Jane Doe,
      Plaintiff,

vs.   CASE NO: <u>99-2306</u>

John Smith,
      Defendant.

JUDGMENT OF PATERNITY

    This matter coming on to be heard and being heard before the undersigned Judge of the <u> Circuit Court </u>, <u> Columbia </u> County, <u> Superior </u>, on the <u>13th</u> day of <u> May </u>, <u>2003</u>, upon the <u> Complaint for Paternity </u> filed in the above-entitled action;

    And it appearing to the Court that the Plaintiff / ~~Petitioner~~ was present in court and proceeding pro se and that the Defendant / ~~Respondent~~ was in court and proceeding pro se / ~~represented by legal counsel~~.

    Upon hearing testimony herein and upon considering the verified pleading of the Plaintiff / ~~Petitioner~~, matters contained in the court file and other evidence introduced by the parties, the Court makes and enters the following:

FINDINGS OF FACT AND CONCLUSIONS OF LAW

    1. All parties are properly before the Court and the Court has jurisdiction over the parties and the subject matter.

    2. The Plaintiff /x~~Petitioner~~ is a citizen and resident of <u> Columbia </u> County, <u> Superior </u>.

    3. The Defendant x~~Respondent~~ is a citizen and resident of <u> Columbia </u> County, <u> Superior </u>.

4. Based upon the results of scientific testing, and other evidence presented at hearing, the parties are the biological parents of ___1___ minor child(~~ren~~): __Veronica Doe__

_____,

born on ___February 14, 2003___ ~~respectively~~

5. The [Plaintiff / ~~Petitioner~~][~~Defendant/Respondent~~] is a fit and proper person to have the care, custody, and control of the minor child(~~ren~~) and it is in the child(~~ren~~)'s best interest to award the Plaintiff / Petitioner custody.

6. The [~~Plaintiff/Petitioner~~] [Defendant /~~Respondent~~] is a fit and proper person to have visitation privileges with the minor child(~~ren~~) and it is in the child(~~ren~~)'s best interest to award the [~~Plaintiff/Petitioner~~] [Defendant /~~Respondent~~] visitation privileges.

7. The [~~Plaintiff/Petitioner~~] [Defendant /~~Respondent~~] is financially able to contribute the sum of $__250.00__ per ___week___ to the support or the minor child(~~ren~~).

IT IS THEREFORE ORDERED, ADJUDGED, AND DECREED THAT:

1. The [~~Plaintiff/Petitioner~~] [Defendant /~~Respondent~~] be declared to be the biological father of the minor child(~~ren~~).

2. The [Plaintiff /~~Petitioner~~][~~Defendant/Respondent~~] be awarded the care, custody, and control of the minor child(~~ren~~).

3. The [~~Plaintiff/Petitioner~~] [Defendant /~~Respondent~~] be awarded visitation with the minor child(~~ren~~) as follows:

Alternate weekends from 7:00 p.m. Friday until 4:00 p.m. Sunday; alternating holidays of New Years Day, Easter,Memorial Day, Fourth of July, Labor Day, Thanksgiving Day, Christmas Eve, and Christmas Day; every Father's Day; and one week during summer vacation from sf two-week's notice).

4. The [~~Plaintiff/Petitioner~~] [Defendant /~~Respondent~~] shall pay the sum of $__250.00__ per ___week___ for the support and maintenance of the minor child(ren).

5. The Plaintiff XXXXXXXXand the Defendant XXXXXXXXXX have an affirmative duty to maintain a suitable and proper environment for the minor child(XXX) at such times as the child(XXX) is/XXX in their care.

6. Neither party shall permanently remove the minor child(XXX) from the jurisdiction of this Court without the prior permission of this Court.

This _23rd_ day of _____May_____ , ___2003_.

Barry D. Hatchett

Judge

CIVIL COVER SHEET

The civil cover sheet and the information contained herein neither replace nor supplement the filing and service of pleadings or other papers as required by law. This form is required for the use of the Clerk of Court for the purposes of reporting judicial workload data pursuant to section 21.005, Superior Statutes Annotated.

I.   CASE STYLE

Jane Doe
Plaintiff/~~Petitioner~~X

vs.

John Smith
Defendant/~~Respondent~~

Case No. ___99-35678___

Division: ___L___

II.   TYPE OF CASE   (Place an X in one box only. If the case fits more than one type of case, select the most definite.)

Domestic Relations

- ❏ Divorce
- ❏ Domestic Violence
- ☒ Paternity
- ❏ Child Support
- ❏ Custody
- ❏ Visitation
- ❏ Other domestic relations

Torts

- ❏ Professional Malpractice
- ❏ Products Liability
- ❏ Auto Negligence
- ❏ Other Negligence

Other Civil

- ❏ Contracts
- ❏ Real Property/ Mortgage Foreclosure
- ❏ Eminent Domain
- ❏ Other

III.   IS JURY TRIAL DEMANDED IN COMPLAINT?
❏ Yes   ☒ No

240

DATE___March, 19, 2003_____

_Jane Doe_____
SIGNATURE OF ATTORNEY OR PARTY
INITIATING ACTION:

Name: ___Jane Doe_____
Address: ___127 Walnut Street_____
_____Superior City, SU 99999____
Phone: ____222-555-5155_____

APPENDIX C: RESOURCES

WEBSITES

About.com Single Parents
http://singleparents.about.com/
parenting/singleparents/

Air Force Family Separation and Readiness (tips for visitation for military families)
www.afcrossroads.com/
famseparation/ret_parent.cfm

Celebrating Children: Single African American Parenting
www.celebratingchildren.com/
archives-singleparenting.html

Christian Single Parents Network
www.cspn.org

www.childcustody.org

Child Custody Resources
www.custody911.com

Child Custody: Single Parent Discussion Forum
www.winchildcustody.com/
singleparent/

Co-Parenting During Summer Vacation Tips
http://ceinfo.unh.edu/Common/
Documents/gsc6600.htm

Dads at a Distance
www.daads.com

Discussion Board for Custodial Parents
www.mafiaboard.com/forum/

Fathers Are Parents Too
www.fapt.org

Fathers Network
www.fathersnetwork.org

Federal Office of Child Support Enforcement
www.acf.dhhs.gov/programs/cse/
index.html

Gay and Lesbian Parenting Links
http://singleparents.about.com/cs/
gaylesbiparents/index/

Grandparents' Visitation Rights
www.grandtimes.com/visit.html

Moms Over Miles
www.momsovermiles.com

National Adoption Information Clearinghouse
www.calib.com/naic/

National Organization of Single Mothers
www.singlemothers.org

Parents Without Partners
www.parentswithoutpartners.org

Parenting Monthly: Tips for Fathers
www.parentingmonthly.org/
dads_info.html

Parenting Teens
www.parentingteens.com

Parenting Today's Teen: Single Parenting Information
www.parentingteens.com/
snglpntgarchive.shtml

Paternity by Choice
www.paternitybychoice.com

Paternity Information Page
www.peak.org/~jedwards/
paternity.html

Paternity Issues
www.vix.com/men/
child-support/paternity.html

Responsible Single Fathers
www.singlefather.org

Single Dads' Index
www.vix.com/pub/men/
single-dad.html

Single Mother Resources
www.singlemomz.com

Single Parent Central
www.singleparentcentral.com/
index.htm

Single Parent Tips
www.singleparent.lifetips.com/
OurGurus.asp

Single Parents Network
www.singleparentsnetwork.com

Single Parents World
www.parentsworld.com

Supervised Visitation Network
www.svnetwork.net

Unmarried Parents Concerns
www.consumeraffairs.com/parenting/
unmarried.html

Youth Behavioral Issues
www.notmykid.org

ORGANIZATIONS

Alliance for Non-Custodial Parents' Rights
P.O. Box 883
Midvale, UT 84047
202-478-1736
www.ancpr.org

Alternatives to Marriage Project
P.O. Box 991010
Boston, MA 02199
781-793-0296
www.unmarried.org

American Association for Single People
P.O. Box 65756
Los Angeles, CA 90065-0765
818-242-5100
www.singlesrights.com

American Coalition for Fathers and Children
1718 Main Street NW, Suite 187
Washington, DC 20036
800-978-DADS
www.acfc.org

Children's Rights Council
6200 Editors Park Drive, Suite 103
Hyattsville, MD 20782
301-559-7563
www.gocrc.com

National Association of Custodial Parents
7501 W. Florence Lane, Suite 102
Boise, ID 83704
www.cphelp.org/natassn.html

National Center for Missing and Exploited Children (NCMEC)
Charles B. Wang International
Children's Building
699 Prince St.
Alexandria, VA 22314-3175
800-THE-LOST
(800-843-5678)
703-274-3900
www.missingkids.com

National Clearinghouse for Alcohol and Drug Information (NCADI)
P.O. Box 2345
Rockville, MD 20847-2345
301-468-2600
800-729-6686
www.health.org

National Clearinghouse on Child Abuse and Neglect Information
330 C Street, S.W.
Washington, DC 20447
800-FYI-3366
703-385-7565
nccanch@calib.com
/www.calib.com/nccanch

Parents Anonymous
675 West Foothill Blvd.
Suite 220
Claremont, CA 91711-3475
909-621-6184
www.parentsanonymous.org

Parents Without Partners
1650 South Dixie Highway, Suite 510
Boca Raton, FL 33432
561-391-8833
www.parentswithoutpartners.org

Single and Custodial Father's Network, Inc.
608 Hastings Road
Pittsburgh, PA 15206
412-665-5940
www.scfn.org

Single Parents Association
4727 E. Bell Road, Suite 45
PMB 209
Phoenix, AZ 85032
623-581-7445
www.singleparents.org

GENETIC TESTING LABORATORIES

American Red Cross Blood Services
Badger-Hawkeye Region
Parentage Laboratory
4880 Sheboygan Avenue
Madison, Wisconsin 53705
608-227-1239

Analytical Genetic Testing Center, Inc.
7808 Cherry Creek Drive South, #201
Denver, CO 80231
303-750-2023

Applied Genetics Inc
201 Summit View Drive, Suite 100
Brentwood, TN 37027
615-889-0444

Baltimore RH Typing Laboratory
400 West Franklin Street
Baltimore, MD 21201
410-225-9595

Blood Bank of San Bernardino and Riverside Counties
399 Blood Bank Road
San Bernardino, CA 92408
714-885-6503

Blood Center of Southeastern Wisconsin
638 North 18th Street
P.O. Box 2178
Milwaukee, WI 53201-2178
414-937-6206

Brotman Medical Center
Blood Bank
3828 Delmas Terrace
Culver City, CA 90230
213-836-7000, ext 2350

Chinatown Medical Laboratory, Inc
1239 Stockton Street
San Francisco, CA 94133
415-956-5481

Clinical Genetics Center
Specialty Diagnostics, Inc
14241 E. Imperial Highway, #C
La Mirada, CA 90638
213-941-6796

Clinical Testing and Research
20 Wilsey Square
Ridgewood, NJ 07450
201-652-2088

Fairfax Identity Laboratories
3025 Hamaker Court, Suite 203
Fairfax, VA 22031
800-848-4362
800-482-3025

Fong Diagnostic Laboratory
7237 East Southgate Drive, Suite 37
Sacramento, Ca 95823
916-421-4167

Gene Prints
P.O. Box 278
Seal Beach, CA 90740
213-594-5947

Gene Proof Technologies
187 Graylynn Drive
Nashville, TN 37214
800-844-7851

Genetic Profiles Corporation
1060 Joshua Way
Vista, CA 92083
800-551-7763

GeneScreen, Inc.
2600 Stemmons Fwy., Suite 133
Dallas, Texas 75207
800-362-8378

GeneScreen, Inc.
5698 Springboro Pike
Dayton, Ohio 45449
800-362-8378

GeneScreen
7237 E. Southgate Drive
Sacramento, CA 95823
800-734-3664

Genetics and IVF Institute
3025 Hamaker Court, Suite 203
Fairfax, VA 22031
800-848-4362

Genetic Design, Inc.
7019 Albert Pick Road, Suite H
Greensboro, NC 27409
800-247-9540

Gentrix, Inc.
1350 South Loop Road, Suite 100
Alameda, CA 94501

Great Lakes Laboratories
118 East 8th Street
Michigan City, IN 46360
800-223-4549

Identity Genetics, Inc.
801 32nd Avenue
Brookings, SD 57006
800-861-1054

Immunological Association of Denver
717 Yosemite Circle
Denver, CO 80206-0351
303-365-9000

Indiana University Medical Genetics Services, Inc.
975 W. Walnut Street, 1B-130
Indianapolis, In 46202-5251
317-274-1075

Irvin Memorial Blood Center
Scientific Services
270 Masonic Avenue
San Francisco, CA 94118
415-567-7400, ext. 448

LabCorp, Inc.
P.O. Box 2230
Burlington, NC 27216-2230
800-743-3944

Laboratory Corporation of America
1330 York Court Extension
Burlington, NC 27215
800-742-3944

LabCorp, Inc.
P.O. Box 2200
1440 York Court Extension
Burlington, NC 27215
800-334-5161

LabCorp, Inc.
1500 Caton Center Drive
Suite N
Arbutus, MD 21227
410-876-6959

LifeCodes
1400 Donelson Pike, Suite A
Nashville, TN 37217
615-360-5000

LifeCodes East Lansing Division
2248 Mt. Hope
Okemos, MI 48864
517-349-3890

Long Beach Genetics
San Jacinto Center
Austin, Texas 78707
800-824-2699

Long Beach Genetics
201 Summit View Drive, #100
Brentwood, TN 37027
800-844-7851

Long Beach Genetics/Esoterix, Inc.
2384 East Pacifica Place
Rancho Dominquez, CA 90220
800-824-2699

Madera Community Hospital Laboratory
1250 East Almond Avenue
Madera, CA 93637
209-673-4485

Memorial Blood Centers of Minnesota, Inc.
2304 Park Avenue
Minneapolis, MN 55404-3789
800-982-9134

Memorial Medical Center of Long Beach
2801 Atlantic Avenue
Long Beach, CA 90806
213-595-3943

Micro Diagnostics
1400 Donelson Pike, Suite A15
Nashville, TN 37217
888-256-6383

Molecular Pathology Laboratory
424 E Church Avenue
Maryville, TN 37804
800-932-2943

National Legal Laboratories
2947 Eyde Parkway
East Lansing, MI 48823
800-837-1504

National Legal Laboratories
2248 East Mount Hope
Okemos, MI 48864
800-837-1504

Paternity Testing Corporation
3501 Berrywood Drive
Columbia, MO 65201

Pathological and Clinical Services
2111 E. Dakota Avenue
P.O. Box 11866
Fresno, CA 93775
209-226-3551

Reliagene Technologies, Inc.
5525 Mounes Street, Suite 101
New Orleans, LA 70123
800-256-4106

Roberts Medical Group
Laboratory
1808 Verdugo Boulevard
Glendale, CA 92108
818-790-4188

Roche Biomedical Laboratories
1447 York Court
Burlington, NC 27215
800-334-5161

Sci Med Consultants
489 Knickerbocker Road
Tenafly, New Jersey 07670

UC San Francisco
Immunogenetics Laboratory
Room HSE
520 Parnassus Avenue
San Francisco, CA 94143
415-476-3883

University of Puerto Rico
Pathology Department
HLA Laboratory
G.P.O. Box 29134
San Juan, PR 00929-0134

University of Utah Diagnostic
Laboratory
729 Arapeen Drive
Building 888, Room 150
Salt Lake City, Utah 94108
801-585-3892

University of North Texas Health
Science Center
3500 Camp Bowie Boulevard
Fort Worth, Texas 76107
800-687-5301

STATE-SPECIFIC RESOURCES

◆ ALABAMA
Alabama Department of
Human Resources
Child Support Enforcement Division
P.O. Box 304000
Montgomery, Alabama 36130-4000
Phone: 334-242-9300
Fax: 334-242-0606
www.dhr.state.al.us

◆ ALASKA
Alaska Child Support
Enforcement Division
Phone: 1-907-269-6900
Toll Free: 800-478-3300
www.csed.state.ak.us

◆ ARIZONA
Arizona Department of
Economic Security
Division of Child Support
Enforcement
Toll Free: 800-882-4151
www.de.state.az.us

◆ ARKANSAS
Arkansas Department of Finance
and Administration
Office of Child Support
Enforcement
400 E Capitol
P.O. Box 8133
Little Rock, Arkansas 72203
Phone: 501-682-6195
Fax: 501-682-6002
www.state.ar.us

◆ CALIFORNIA
California Department of Child
Support Services
P.O. Box 419064
Rancho Cordova, California
95741-9064
Phone: 866-249-0773
Fax: 916-464-5065
www.childsup.cahwnet.gov

◆ **COLORADO**
Colorado Department of
Human Services
Division of Child Support
Enforcement
1575 Sherman Street
Denver, Colorado 80203-1714
Phone: 303-866-5700
Fax: 303-866-4047
www.childsupport.state.co.us

◆ **CONNECTICUT**
Connecticut Department of
Social Services
25 Sigourney Street
Hartford, Connecticut 06106-5033
Toll Free: 800-842-1508
www.dss.state.ct.us

◆ **DELAWARE**
Delaware Health and
Social Services
Division of Child Support
Enforcement
P.O. Box 904
New Castle, DE 19720
Phone: 302-577-7171
www.state.de.us

◆ **DISTRICT OF COLUMBIA**
Child Support
Enforcement Division
441 4th Street, NW, Suite 550 N
Washington, D.C. 20001
Phone: 202-442-9900
www.csed.dc.gov

◆ **FLORIDA**
Florida Child Support
Enforcement
Toll Free: 800-622-KIDS (5437)
Dade County: 305-503-2740
Manatee: 941-741-4039
www.myflorida.com

◆ **GEORGIA**
Office of Child Support
Enforcement
Toll Free: 800-227-7993
Phone: 404-657-2780
www.cse.dhr.state.ga.us

◆ **HAWAII**
Department of the
Attorney General
Child Support Enforcement Agency
Toll Free: 888-317-9081
www.ehawaii.gov

◆ **IDAHO**
Department of
Health and Welfare
450 West State Street, 10th Floor
P.O. Box 83720
Boise, Idaho 83720-0036
Phone: 208-334-5500
Fax: 208-334-6558
www.idaho.gov

◆ **ILLINOIS**
Illinois Department of Public Aid
Child Support Enforcement
Help Line: 800-447-4278
Phone: 217-785-1692
www.illinois.gov

◆ **INDIANA**
Indiana Family and Social
Services Administration
Bureau of Child Support
P.O. Box 7083
402 W Washington Street
Indianapolis, Indiana 46207-7083
Child Support Hotline: 800-926-8336
www.in.gov

◆ **IOWA**
Iowa Department of
Human Services
Hoover State Office Building
Des Moines, Iowa 50319
Toll Free: 800-972-2017
www.dhs.state.ia.us

◆ **KANSAS**
**Kansas Department of Social
and Rehabilitation Services**
Child Support Enforcement
915 SW Harrison Street
Topeka, Kansas 66612
Phone: 785-296-3959/
785-296-2173
www.srskansas.org

◆ **KENTUCKY**
Office of the Attorney General
Child Support Enforcement Division
The Capitol, Suite 118
700 Capitol Avenue
Frankfort, Kentucky 40601-3449
Phone: 502-696-5300
www.kyattorneygeneral.com

◆ **LOUISIANA**
Department of Social Services
Child Support Enforcement Services
530 Lakeland Avenue
Baton Rouge, LA 70804
Phone: 225-342-4780
Fax: 225-342-7397
www.dss.state.la.us

◆ **MAINE**
Department of Human Services
Division of Support Enforcement
and Recovery
11 SHS Whitten Road
Augusta, Maine 04333
Phone: 207-287-3110
Fax: 207-287-2334
www.state.me.us

◆ **MARYLAND**
**Department of
Human Resources**
Child Support Enforcement
Administration
311 West Saratoga Street
Baltimore, MD 21201
Toll Free: 800-332-6347
www.dhr.state.md.us

◆ **MASSACHUSETTS**
**Child Support Enforcement
Division**
51 Sleeper Street
Boston, MA 02210
Toll Free: 800-332-2733
www.state.ma.us/cse

◆ **MICHIGAN**
Family Independence Agency
P.O. Box 30037
Lansing, Michigan 48909
Phone: 517-373-2035
Fax: 517-335-6101
www.michigan.gov/fia

◆ **MINNESOTA**
Department of Human Services
Child Support Enforcement
444 Lafayette Road North
St Paul, Minnesota 55155
Phone: 651-296-2542
www.dhs.state.mn.us

◆ **MISSISSIPPI**
**Mississippi Department of
Human Services**
Division of Child Support
Enforcement
750 North State Street
Jackson, Mississippi 39205
Toll Free: 800-948-4010
www.mdhs.state.ms.us

◆ **MISSOURI**
Department of Social Services
Division of Child Support
Enforcement
E-mail: askcse@mail.state.mo.us
Toll Free: 800-859-7999
www.dss.state.mo.us

◆ **NEBRASKA**
Health and Human Services
Child Support Enforcement
P.O. Box 94728
Lincoln, NE 68509-4728
Toll Free: 877-631-9973
Phone: 402-441-8715
www.hhs.state.ne.us

◆ **NEVADA**
Department of Human
Resources
Welfare Division–Child Support
Enforcement
505 East King Street
Carson City, Nevada 89701-3708
Phone: 775-684-4000
www.welfare.state.nv.us

◆ **NEW HAMPSHIRE**
Department of Health and
Human Services
NH DHHS Commissioners Office
129 Pleasant Street
Concord, NH 03301-3857
Toll Free: 800-852-3345
www.dhhs.state.nh.us

◆ **NEW JERSEY**
Department of Human Services
Child Support Hotline: 877-655-4371
www.njchildsupport.org

◆ **NEW MEXICO**
Child Support Enforcement
Division
P.O. Box 25110
Santa Fe, NM 87504
Toll Free Within NM: 800-288-7207
Toll Free Outside NM:
800-585-7631
http://childsupport.hsd.state.nm.us

◆ **NEW YORK**
New York State Office of
Temporary and Disability
Assistance
40 North Pearl Street
Albany, New York 12243
Toll Free: 800-846-0773
www.otda.state.ny.us

◆ **NORTH CAROLINA**
Department of Health and
Human Services
Child Support Enforcement
P.O. Box 20800
Raleigh, NC 27619-0800
Toll Free: 800-992-9457
www.dhhs.state.nc.us

◆ **NORTH DAKOTA**
Department of Human Services
Child Support Enforcement
1929 N Washington Street
P.O. Box 7190
Bismark, ND 58507-7190
Toll Free: 800-366-6888
www.childsupportnd.com

◆ **OHIO**
Office of Child Support
Ohio Department of Job and
Family Services
30 E Broad Street, 31st Floor
Columbus, Ohio 43215-3414
Phone: 614-752-6561
Fax: 614-752-9760
www.state.oh.us

◆ **OKLAHOMA**
Department of Human Services
P.O. Box 53552
Oklahoma City, Oklahoma 73152
KIDS LINE: 800-522-2922
www.okdhs.org

◆ **OREGON**
Oregon Department of Human Services
Children, Adult, Families
500 Summer Street, NE E62
Salem, Oregon 97301-1067
Phone: 503-945-5651
Fax: 503-373-7032
www.afs.hr.state.or.us

◆ **PENNSYLVANIA**
Department of Public Welfare
Health and Welfare Building
P.O. Box 2675
Harrisburg, PA 17105-2675
Child Support Helpline:
800-932-0211
www.dpw.state.pa.us

◆ **RHODE ISLAND**
Department of Administration
Division of Taxation—Child Support
Enforcement
77 Dorrance Street
Providence, Rhode Island 02930
Phone: 401-222-3845
www.childsupportliens.com

◆ **SOUTH CAROLINA**
**Department of Social Services—
Child Support Enforcement**
P.O. Box 1469
Columbia, South Carolina
29202-1469
Toll Free: 800-768-5858
www.state.sc.us/dss

◆ **SOUTH DAKOTA**
**Department of Social Services—
Child Support Enforcement**
700 Governors Drive
Pierre, South Dakota 57501
Phone: 605-773-3641
www.state.sd.us

◆ **TENNESSEE**
Department of Human Services
400 Deaderick Street
Nashville, Tennessee 37248
Toll Free: 800-838-6911
www.state.tn.us

◆ **TEXAS**
Office of Attorney General
P.O. Box 12548
Austin, Texas 78711-2548
Toll Free: 800-252-8014
Phone: 512-460-6000
www.oag.state.tx.us

◆ **UTAH**
Department of Human Services
Office of Recovery Services
515 East 100 South
Salt Lake City, Utah 84102
Toll Free: 800-662-8525
www.ors.state.ut.us

◆ **VERMONT**
Office of Child Support
Vermont Agency of Human Services
103 South Main Street
Waterbury, Vermont 05671-1901
Toll Free: 800-786-3214
www.ocs.state.vt.us

◆ **VIRGINIA**
Department of Social Services
Child Support Enforcement
730 East Broad Street
Richmond, Virginia 23219
Phone: 804-692-1900
www.dss.state.va.us

◆ **WASHINGTON**
Department of Social and Health Services
Division of Child Support
P.O. Box 9162
Olympia, WA 98507-9162
Toll Free: 800-457-6202
www.wa.gov

◆ WEST VIRGINIA
**Department of Health and
Human Services**
Bureau for Child Support
Enforcement
Toll Free: 800-249-3778
www.wvdhhr.org

◆ WISCONSIN
**Wisconsin Department of
Workforce Development**
Bureau of Child Support
201 E Washington Avenue
Madison, Wisconsin 53702
Phone: 608-267-4337
www.dwd.state.wi.us

◆ WYOMING
Child Support Enforcement
2300 Capitol Avenue
3rd Floor
Cheyenne, Wyoming 82002-0490
Phone: 307-777-6948
www.state.wy.us

INDEX

ABOUT THE AUTHOR

Jacqueline D. Stanley received her law degree from Wake Forest University. Ms. Stanley has coauthored many self-help legal guides, including *How to File for Divorce in North Carolina*. She currently resides in Greensboro, North Carolina.

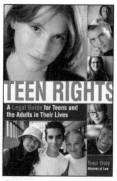
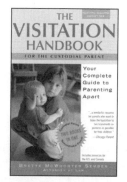

SPHINX® PUBLISHING'S STATE TITLES
Up-to-Date for Your State

CALIFORNIA

CA Power of Attorney Handbook (2E)	$18.95
How to File for Divorce in CA (3E)	$26.95
How to Make a CA Will	$16.95
How to Probate and Settle an Estate in CA	$26.95
How to Start a Business in CA	$18.95
How to Win in Small Claims Court in CA	$16.95
The Landlord's Legal Guide in CA	$24.95

FLORIDA

Florida Power of Attorney Handbook (2E)	$16.95
How to File for Divorce in FL (7E)	$26.95
How to Form a Corporation in FL (5E)	$24.95
How to Form a Limited Liability Company in FL (2E)	$24.95
How to Form a Partnership in FL	$22.95
How to Make a FL Will (6E)	$16.95
How to Modify Your FL Divorce Judgement (4E)	$24.95
How to Probate and Settle an Estate in FL (4E)	$26.95
How to Start a Business in FL (5E)	$16.95
How to Win in Small Claims Court in FL (7E)	$18.95
Land Trusts in Florida (6E)	$29.95
Landlords' Rights and Duties in FL (8E)	$21.95

GEORGIA

How to File for Divorce in GA (4E)	$21.95
How to Make a GA Will (4E)	$21.95
How to Start a Business in GA (2E)	$16.95

ILLINOIS

Child Custody, Visitation, and Support in IL	$24.95
How to File for Divorce in IL (3E)	$24.95
How to Make an IL Will (3E)	$16.95
How to Start a Business in IL (2E)	$18.95
The Landlord's Legal Guide in IL	$24.95

MASSACHUSETTS

How to File for Divorce in MA (3E)	$24.95
How to Form a Corporation in MA	$24.95
How to Make a MA Will (2E)	$16.95
How to Start a Business in MA (2E)	$18.95
The Landlord's Legal Guide in MA	$24.95

MICHIGAN

How to File for Divorce in MI (2E)	$21.95
How to Make a MI Will (3E)	$16.95
How to Start a Business in MI (3E)	$18.95

Sphinx Publishing's Legal Survival Guides are directly available from the publisher, or from your local bookstores.

MINNESOTA

How to File for Divorce in MN	$21.95
How to Form a Corporation in MN	$24.95
How to Make a MN Will (2E)	$16.95

NEW JERSEY

How to File for Divorce in NJ	$24.95

NEW YORK

Child Custody, Visitation and Support in NY	$26.95
How to File for Divorce in NY (2E)	$26.95
How to Form a Corporation in NY (2E)	$24.95
How to Make a NY Will (2E)	$16.95
How to Start a Business in NY (2E)	$18.95
How to Win in Small Claims Court in NY (2E)	$18.95
Landlords' Legal Guide in NY	$24.95
New York Power of Attorney Handbook	$19.95
Tenants' Rights in NY	$21.95

NORTH CAROLINA

How to File for Divorce in NC (3E)	$22.95
How to Make a NC Will (3E)	$16.95
How to Start a Business in NC (3E)	$18.95
Landlords' Rights & Duties in NC	$21.95

OHIO

How to File for Divorce in OH, 2E	$24.95
How to Form a Corporation in OH	$24.95
How to Make an OH Will	$16.95

PENNSYLVANIA

Child Custody, Visitation and Support in PA	$26.95
How to File for Divorce in PA (3E)	$26.95
How to Make a PA Will (2E)	$16.95
How to Start a Business in PA (2E)	$18.95
The Landlord's Legal Guide in PA	$24.95

TEXAS

Child Custody, Visitation, and Support in TX	$22.95
How to File for Divorce in TX (3E)	$24.95
How to Form a Corporation in TX (2E)	$24.95
How to Make a TX Will (3E)	$16.95
How to Probate and Settle an Estate in TX (3E)	$26.95
How to Start a Business in TX (3E)	$18.95
How to Win in Small Claims Court in TX (2E)	$16.95
Landlords' Rights and Duties in TX (2E)	$21.95

For credit card orders call 1–800–432-7444,
write P.O. Box 4410, Naperville, IL 60567-4410, or fax 630-961-2168

SPHINX® PUBLISHING'S NATIONAL TITLES
Valid in All 50 States

LEGAL SURVIVAL IN BUSINESS

The Complete Book of Corporate Forms	$24.95
How to Form a Limited Liability Company	$22.95
Incorporate in Delaware from Any State	$24.95
Incorporate in Nevada from Any State	$24.95
How to Form a Nonprofit Corporation (2E)	$24.95
How to Form Your Own Corporation (3E)	$24.95
How to Form Your Own Partnership (2E)	$24.95
How to Register Your Own Copyright (4E)	$24.95
How to Register Your Own Trademark (3E)	$21.95
Most Valuable Corporate Forms You'll Ever Need (3E)	$21.95
The Small Business Owner's Guide to Bankruptcy	$21.95

LEGAL SURVIVAL IN COURT

Crime Victim's Guide to Justice (2E)	$21.95
Grandparents' Rights (3E)	$24.95
Help Your Lawyer Win Your Case (2E)	$14.95
Jurors' Rights (2E)	$12.95
Legal Research Made Easy (3E)	$21.95
Winning Your Personal Injury Claim (2E)	$24.95
Your Rights When You Owe Too Much	$16.95

LEGAL SURVIVAL IN REAL ESTATE

Essential Guide to Real Estate Contracts	$18.95
Essential Guide to Real Estate Leases	$18.95
How to Buy a Condominium or Townhome (2E)	$19.95

LEGAL SURVIVAL IN PERSONAL AFFAIRS

The 529 College Savings Plan	$16.95
The Complete Legal Guide to Senior Care	$21.95
How to File Your Own Bankruptcy (5E)	$21.95
How to File Your Own Divorce (4E)	$24.95
How to Make Your Own Simple Will (3E)	$18.95
How to Write Your Own Living Will (3E)	$18.95
How to Write Your Own Premarital Agreement (3E)	$24.95
Living Trusts and Other Ways to Avoid Probate (3E)	$24.95
Mastering the MBE	$16.95
Most Valuable Personal Legal Forms You'll Ever Need	$24.95
Neighbor v. Neighbor (2E)	$16.95
The Nanny and Domestic Help Legal Kit	$22.95
The Power of Attorney Handbook (4E)	$19.95
Repair Your Own Credit and Deal with Debt	$18.95
Sexual Harassment: Your Guide to Legal Action	$18.95
The Social Security Benefits Handbook (3E)	$18.95
Social Security Q&A	$12.95
Teen Rights	$22.95
Unmarried Parents' Rights	$19.95
U.S. Immigration Step By Step	$21.95
U.S.A. Immigration Guide (4E)	$24.95
The Visitation Handbook	$18.95
Win Your Unemployment Compensation Claim (2E)	$21.95
Your Right to Child Custody, Visitation, and Support (2E)	$24.95

LEGAL SURVIVAL IN SPANISH

Cómo Hacer su Propio Testamento	$16.95
Cómo Restablecer su propio Crédito y Renegociar sus Deudas	$21.95
Cómo Solicitar su Propio Divorcio	$24.95
Guía de Inmigración a Estados Unidos (3E)	$24.95
Guía de Justicia para Víctimas del Crimen	$21.95
Manual de Beneficios para el Seguro Social	$18.95

SPHINX® PUBLISHING ORDER FORM

BILL TO:			SHIP TO:			
Phone #		Terms	F.O.B.	Chicago, IL		Ship Date

Charge my: ☐ VISA ☐ MasterCard ☐ American Express ☐ **Money Order or Personal Check**

Credit Card Number   **Expiration Date**

Qty	ISBN	Title	Retail
		SPHINX PUBLISHING NATIONAL TITLES	
____	1-57248-148-X	Cómo Hacer su Propio Testamento	$16.95
____	1-57248-226-5	Cómo Restablecer su propio Crédito y Renegociar sus Deudas	$21.95
____	1-57248-147-1	Cómo Solicitar su Propio Divorcio	$24.95
____	1-57248-238-9	The 529 College Savings Plan	$16.95
____	1-57248-166-8	The Complete Book of Corporate Forms	$24.95
____	1-57248-229-X	The Complete Legal Guide to Senior Care	$21.95
____	1-57248-163-3	Crime Victim's Guide to Justice (2E)	$21.95
____	1-57248-159-5	Essential Guide to Real Estate Contracts	$18.95
____	1-57248-160-9	Essential Guide to Real Estate Leases	$18.95
____	1-57248-139-0	Grandparents' Rights (3E)	$24.95
____	1-57248-188-9	Guia de Inmigración a Estados Unidos (3E)	$24.95
____	1-57248-187-0	Guia de Justicia para Victimas del Crimen	$21.95
____	1-57248-103-X	Help Your Lawyer Win Your Case (2E)	$14.95
____	1-57248-164-1	How to Buy a Condominium or Townhome (2E)	$19.95
____	1-57248-191-9	How to File Your Own Bankruptcy (5E)	$21.95
____	1-57248-132-3	How to File Your Own Divorce (4E)	$24.95
____	1-57248-083-1	How to Form a Limited Liability Company	$22.95
____	1-57248-231-1	How to Form a Nonprofit Corporation (2E)	$24.95
____	1-57248-133-1	How to Form Your Own Corporation (3E)	$24.95
____	1-57248-224-9	How to Form Your Own Partnership (2E)	$24.95
____	1-57248-232-X	How to Make Your Own Simple Will (3E)	$18.95
____	1-57248-200-1	How to Register Your Own Copyright (4E)	$24.95
____	1-57248-104-8	How to Register Your Own Trademark (3E)	$21.95
____	1-57248-233-8	How to Write Your Own Living Will (3E)	$18.95
____	1-57248-156-0	How to Write Your Own Premarital Agreement (3E)	$24.95
____	1-57248-230-3	Incorporate in Delaware from Any State	$24.95
____	1-57248-158-7	Incorporate in Nevada from Any State	$24.95
____	1-57071-333-2	Jurors' Rights (2E)	$12.95
____	1-57248-223-0	Legal Research Made Easy (3E)	$21.95
____	1-57248-165-X	Living Trusts and Other Ways to Avoid Probate (3E)	$24.95
____	1-57248-186-2	Manual de Beneficios para el Seguro Social	$18.95
____	1-57248-220-6	Mastering the MBE	$16.95
____	1-57248-167-6	Most Valuable Bus. Legal Forms You'll Ever Need (3E)	$21.95

Qty	ISBN	Title	Retail
____	1-57248-130-7	Most Valuable Personal Legal Forms You'll Ever Need	$24.95
____	1-57248-098-X	The Nanny and Domestic Help Legal Kit	$22.95
____	1-57248-089-0	Neighbor v. Neighbor (2E)	$16.95
____	1-57248-169-2	The Power of Attorney Handbook (4E)	$19.95
____	1-57248-149-8	Repair Your Own Credit and Deal with Debt	$18.95
____	1-57248-217-6	Sexual Harassment: Your Guide to Legal Action	$18.95
____	1-57248-219-2	The Small Business Owner's Guide to Bankruptcy	$21.95
____	1-57248-168-4	The Social Security Benefits Handbook (3E)	$18.95
____	1-57248-216-8	Social Security Q&A	$12.95
____	1-57248-221-4	Teen Rights	$22.95
____	1-57071-399-5	Unmarried Parents' Rights	$19.95
____	1-57248-218-4	U.S. Immigration Step-by-Step	$21.95
____	1-57248-161-7	U.S.A. Immigration Guide (4E)	$24.95
____	1-57248-192-7	The Visitation Handbook	$18.95
____	1-57248-225-7	Win Your Unemployment Compensation Claim (2E)	$21.95
____	1-57248-138-2	Winning Your Personal Injury Claim (2E)	$24.95
____	1-57248-162-5	Your Right to Child Custody, Visitation, and Support (2E)	$24.95
____	1-57248-157-9	Your Rights When You Owe Too Much	$16.95
		CALIFORNIA TITLES	
____	1-57248-150-1	CA Power of Attorney Handbook (2E)	$18.95
____	1-57248-151-X	How to File for Divorce in CA (3E)	$26.95
____	1-57071-356-1	How to Make a CA Will	$16.95
____	1-57248-145-5	How to Probate and Settle and Estate in CA	$26.95
____	1-57248-146-3	How to Start a Business in CA	$18.95
____	1-57248-194-3	How to Win in Small Claims Court in CA (2E)	$18.95
____	1-57248-196-X	The Landlord's Legal Guide in CA	$24.95
		FLORIDA TITLES	
____	1-57071-363-4	Florida Power of Attorney Handbook (2E)	$16.95
____	1-57248-176-5	How to File for Divorce in FL (7E)	$26.95
____	1-57248-177-3	How to Form a Corporation in FL (5E)	$24.95
____	1-57248-203-6	How to Form a Limited Liability Co. in FL (2E)	$24.95
____	1-57071-401-0	How to Form a Partnership in FL	$22.95

Form Continued on Following Page   **Subtotal** _____

Qty	ISBN	Title	Retail
		FLORIDA TITLES (CONT'D)	
_____	1-57248-113-7	How to Make a FL Will (6E)	$16.95
_____	1-57248-088-2	How to Modify Your FL Divorce Judgment (4E)	$24.95
_____	1-57248-144-7	How to Probate and Settle an Estate in FL (4E)	$26.95
_____	1-57248-081-5	How to Start a Business in FL (5E)	$16.95
_____	1-57248-204-4	How to Win in Small Claims Court in FL (7E)	$18.95
_____	1-57248-202-8	Land Trusts in Florida (6E)	$29.95
_____	1-57248-123-4	Landlords' Rights and Duties in FL (8E)	$21.95
		GEORGIA TITLES	
_____	1-57248-137-4	How to File for Divorce in GA (4E)	$21.95
_____	1-57248-180-3	How to Make a GA Will (4E)	$21.95
_____	1-57248-140-4	How to Start Business in GA (2E)	$16.95
		ILLINOIS TITLES	
_____	1-57248-244-3	Child Custody, Visitation, and Support in IL	$24.95
_____	1-57248-206-0	How to File for Divorce in IL (3E)	$24.95
_____	1-57248-170-6	How to Make an IL Will (3E)	$16.95
_____	1-57248-247-8	How to Start a Business in IL (3E)	$21.95
_____	1-57248-252-4	The Landlord's Legal Guide in IL	$24.95
		MASSACHUSETTS TITLES	
_____	1-57248-128-5	How to File for Divorce in MA (3E)	$24.95
_____	1-57248-115-3	How to Form a Corporation in MA	$24.95
_____	1-57248-108-0	How to Make a MA Will (2E)	$16.95
_____	1-57248-106-4	How to Start a Business in MA (2E)	$18.95
_____	1-57248-209-5	The Landlord's Legal Guide in MA	$24.95
		MICHIGAN TITLES	
_____	1-57248-215-X	How to File for Divorce in MI (3E)	$24.95
_____	1-57248-182-X	How to Make a MI Will (3E)	$16.95
_____	1-57248-183-8	How to Start a Business in MI (3E)	$18.95
		MINNESOTA TITLES	
_____	1-57248-142-0	How to File for Divorce in MN	$21.95
_____	1-57248-179-X	How to Form a Corporation in MN	$24.95
_____	1-57248-178-1	How to Make a MN Will (2E)	$16.95
		NEW JERSEY TITLES	
_____	1-57248-239-7	How to File for Divorce in NJ	$24.95
		NEW YORK TITLES	
_____	1-57248-193-5	Child Custody, Visitation and Support in NY	$26.95
_____	1-57248-141-2	How to File for Divorce in NY (2E)	$26.95

Qty	ISBN	Title	Retail
_____	1-57248-249-4	How to Form a Corporation in NY (2EO)	$24.95
_____	1-57248-095-5	How to Make a NY Will (2E)	$16.95
_____	1-57248-199-4	How to Start a Business in NY (2E)	$18.95
_____	1-57248-198-6	How to Win in Small Claims Court in NY (2E)	$18.95
_____	1-57248-197-8	Landlords' Legal Guide in NY	$24.95
_____	1-57071-188-7	New York Power of Attorney Handbook	$19.95
_____	1-57248-122-6	Tenants' Rights in New York	$21.9*
		NORTH CAROLINA TITLES	
_____	1-57248-185-4	How to File for Divorce in NC (3E)	$22.9*
_____	1-57248-129-3	How to Make a NC Will (3E)	$16.9
_____	1-57248-184-6	How to Start a Business in NC (3E)	$18.9*
_____	1-57248-091-2	Landlords' Rights & Duties in NC	$21.9*
		OHIO TITLES	
_____	1-57248-190-0	How to File for Divorce in OH (2E)	$24.9
_____	1-57248-174-9	How to Form a Corporation in OH	$24.9*
_____	1-57248-173-0	How to Make an OH Will	$16.9*
		PENNSYLVANIA TITLES	
_____	1-57248-242-7	Child Custody, Visitation and Support in PA	$26.9*
_____	1-57248-211-7	How to File for Divorce in PA (3E)	$26.9
_____	1-57248-094-7	How to Make a PA Will (2E)	$16.9
_____	1-57248-112-9	How to Start a Business in PA (2E)	$18.9
_____	1-57248-245-1	The Landlord's Legal Guide in PA	$24.9
		TEXAS TITLES	
_____	1-57248-171-4	Child Custody, Visitation, and Support in TX	$22.9
_____	1-57248-172-2	How to File for Divorce in TX (3E)	$24.9
_____	1-57248-114-5	How to Form a Corporation in TX (2E)	$24.
_____	1-57248-255-9	How to Make a TX Will (3E)	$16.
_____	1-57248-214-1	How to Probate and Settle an Estate in TX (3E)	$26.*
_____	1-57248-228-1	How to Start a Business in TX (3E)	$18.*
_____	1-57248-111-0	How to Win in Small Claims Court in TX (2E)	$16.
_____	1-57248-110-2	Landlords' Rights and Duties in TX (2E)	$21.

SUBTOTAL THIS PAGE _____

SUBTOTAL PREVIOUS PAGE _____

Shipping — $5.00 for 1st book, $1.00 each additional _____

Illinois residents add 6.75% sales tax _____

Connecticut residents add 6.00% sales tax _____

TOTAL _____